Life Not Typical
*How Special Needs Parenting Changed My
Faith and My Song*

JENNIFER
SHAW

This Side Up, LLC
COLUMBUS, OHIO

THIS SIDE UP, LLC

Life Not Typical
Copyright © 2012 by Jennifer Shaw

Scripture taken from the *Holy Bible, New International Version* ®. NIV®. Copyright © 1973, 1978, 1984 by International Bible Society. Used by permission of Zondervan. All rights reserved.

ISBN-10: 0-9839591-0-2
ISBN-13: 978-0-9839591-0-6

Library of Congress Control Number: 2011938111

Cover design: Nathan Colba
Cover photography: Jennifer Shaw

This Side Up, LLC
P.O. Box 340773
Columbus, OH 43234

Printed in the United States of America by Worzalla

To my family

Your courage, humor, perseverance, and faith inspire me every day

Contents

Acknowledgments

There are so many people to thank!

First and foremost, I thank my husband, Nathan. Nathan, you are my rock, my techie genius, and the love of my life. Without you, this book never would have happened. Thank you for all your hard work, and for all the ways you have truly been a man of God and a blessing in my life. How did I get so lucky?

Rinnah and Rachel, you are the best daughters a mother could ever hope to have. You bring joy and laughter into my life everyday. I am so proud of your compassion, love, intelligence, patience, creativity, and sweetness. You are two of the greatest blessings I can imagine.

Toby, you keep me laughing, you amaze me with your brilliance, and I have been reminded again through this book what a fighter you are. You were courageous long before you knew what the word meant. You are my reminder everyday that God is good.

Mom, how can I thank you for all you are to me? You have been a tremendous support in my ministry, you have given me a life-long model of how to walk with the Lord, you have been so brave, and you have loved me even when I'm not lovable. I'm grateful for you.

To my publicist, Gina Adams, thank you for pushing me to write this book and for all of your help in the process. It truly wouldn't have happened without you!

To Patti, thanks for all the prayers! You rock.

To all of my friends, thank you for putting up with the constant talk about this book. I'm sure there is a special reward in heaven for patience.

To Stacey, Katie, and Karen, I cannot thank you enough for your generosity in sharing your time and expertise to provide the interviews for the appendixes. They will help so many families, and your heart for children is amazing.

To all of the professionals at Columbus Speech and Hearing Center, thank you so much for everything you did for our family and for allowing us to use your excellent resources in the back of this book. When even the billing department treats clients as old friends, you know you have a special place.

To the therapists and teachers at Sutter Park Preschool, you became like family to us. We were so grateful to send our child to school everyday knowing that he was truly loved and cared for there. We are thankful for you.

Finally, and most importantly, thanks to God. I cannot even imagine how we would have done these years without You, and I will never stop thanking You for holding our future.

Soli Deo Gloria!

Introduction

As I send this book out into the world, I feel the need to say a few things. The first is simply that I am a parent. I am not a specialist, a therapist, a psychologist, or a member of the medical community. I have learned a lot about the disorder that has profoundly impacted our family, and I have done my best to thoroughly research everything mentioned in this book, but therapies are different for different children and prognoses will vary. If you have a concern for a child in your life, please pursue it with your doctor and the specialists in your area. Hopefully our story will give you a place to start.

I also want to say that writing this book has brought home to me again how very blessed my family has been. We live in an area with tremendous resources for special needs children, our jobs allowed us the flexibility to participate in Toby's therapy, our school district was unusually responsive and helpful, and we experienced amazing miracles due to God's grace and the early intervention of numerous specialists. I do not know why we have experienced the outcome we have when many have not, but I am grateful for God's mercy to us. In a myriad of ways, our circumstances were not typical.

I have talked to so many parents who are dealing with incredibly difficult situations – single parents who are trying to support their families and still get their children the help they need, parents in remote areas where therapy is not accessible, parents living in school districts that simply won't help them, parents who have spent years trying to get a diagnosis, and parents who have had to choose between paying for therapy or buying food for their families. If you are one of those parents, please don't give up. Let our story encourage you to keep pushing, keep seeking, keep advocating for your child. Early intervention is ideal but it is never too late. Gains can be made, lives can be changed, and there is always hope. God is still in control. We know so many families with special needs children, and we see incredible things happen every day which never "should" happen.

As I've spent the last nine months recreating the time period covered in this book, poring over our family journals, blogs, photos, test reports, and therapy plans, one thing has become abundantly clear to me: God loves us. It has been difficult to relive some of the worst moments of my life, and yet, in every hard memory, I have an accompanying memory of God's presence. He has never left me alone. He has been so faithful to me, to my dad, to my son, and to our family. Isaiah 30:18 says, "Yet the Lord longs to be gracious to you; He rises to show you compassion." This same God who carried our family through so many struggles longs to be with you too. I hope you meet Him in these pages.

JENNIFER SHAW
Columbus, Ohio
September 2011

"I have come that they may have life, and have it to the full."
John 10:10b

CHAPTER 1

A Realization

September 2006

I t was a beautiful, sunny day in southeast Florida. We were visiting friends and taking a trip to the beach. Our little girls, Rinnah and Rachel, were chattering excitedly in the back seat and looking forward to this rare treat for our family from Ohio. The beach was one of their favorite places on earth and they would build sandcastles and play in the waves for hours and hours if they could.

I watched as the palm trees waved in the wind, and thought how beautiful it was, but I wasn't enjoying it. I was happy for the girls' sake, but I had a knot in my stomach that would not ease up. The day was windy and the waves were high. This wasn't a gentle beach on a calm day, and I didn't know if that would have helped anyway. In the back of the van, my son, Toby, began to cry softly in his car seat.

I didn't know why he always had this reaction, but it had been this way his whole life, and we knew some of the triggers. I started my usual reassurances. "Don't worry, buddy, Mommy's going to wrap you in a towel. I won't let the wind blow on you. It won't even touch you."

I knew he understood me, but he couldn't respond. At just two years old, he still wasn't making many sounds, and he had no words. My assurances didn't touch him, though, and he just kept whimpering, fearful in a way I never understood.

We stopped the car, and I felt that familiar pit in my stomach. This wasn't going to turn out well.

As we climbed out and started unloading the car, Toby began to cry in earnest. I told my husband, Nathan, to take the girls down to the beach, and Toby and I would follow as soon as we could. I knew in my heart that Toby wanted to be an easy-going, happy kid, but something was preventing him and we didn't know what it was. His behaviors, which had at first only been a bit odd, were escalating, and now had become extreme and frightening.

Nathan took the beach chairs and towels and headed off to the beach with the girls. I tried to calm Toby down, leaving him in the car until the last second, talking to him the whole time. I knew he felt safer in the car, and I knew certain things really scared him. I just didn't know why.

"All right, buddy, I'm going to get you out now. Okay, the belts are off. Don't worry, honey, I won't let the wind touch you. We're going to wrap this towel around you, see? It's going to be fine. Mommy's going to hold you the whole time."

As I pulled Toby from the car, he saw the waves and began to sob. "No, buddy, don't worry! We're not going to get wet. We're not going to touch the water at all. We're not even going to touch the sand. We're just going to sit on a chair and watch your sisters. It will be fun. I'm going to hold you in my lap. The sand won't touch you, the water won't touch you. I'll carry you there. You won't even have to touch the ground. We'll sit on a chair and watch. You'll be safe." Talking continuously, I carried him to the beach.

We sat in a chair under an umbrella, Toby wrapped in a towel with only his little face looking out. I knew somehow that he was terribly afraid of the sand, the water, and the wind. It made no sense, but it was very real to him. He began to panic and cry, terrified and sobbing. My heart just broke for him, and I knew we couldn't stay.

I gave up, and as I stood to go back to the car, I started sobbing with him. It had only been a few weeks since my dad had passed away from Lou Gehrig's disease, and I was so emotionally spent. I grieved for my dad, and now for my son. I'd lost Dad. Were we now going to lose Toby? I just didn't think I could handle one more fight. Toby was shutting down at an alarming pace. He was not eating, not talking, not even wanting to be touched, and I couldn't explain it away anymore.

Many people had said to us over the past months, "Oh, he just has a difficult personality" or "He's just very particular about what he wants" but I knew right then it was none of those things. This was not normal. I couldn't deny it one more day.

There was something really wrong with my baby.

CHAPTER 2

Growing Up

When I was growing up, I always had big plans. I knew from a very early age that I wanted to be a musician. I had a tantrum when I was three years old because I couldn't get the music in my head to come out right on our piano. I begged for lessons and finally got them when I turned six. One day I was a little early for my lesson and the daughter of my teacher was home from college where she was studying piano performance. She was playing a Beethoven sonata and I remember thinking that I didn't care what I had to do or how long I had to work, I was going to play like that someday. Being famous would have been nice too, but it was always more about the music. I wanted to live in the music!

My parents, Dave and Beth Chilcoat, were in full-time Christian ministry and had a very strong faith in God, but when I became a teenager, I didn't want to follow in those footsteps. It seemed to me that I had a pretty good handle on what I wanted out of life and that God had a lot of rules that would prevent me from having much fun or doing what I wanted to do.

When I was fifteen, I told God that I was done following Him. It wasn't that I didn't believe He was real; I actually did. But I knew that God would not approve of the things I wanted to do, so God and I had to be done. I was convinced that I knew how to be happy.

Jennifer at age seven with her dad, Dave Chilcoat

For me, happiness was all about success, and I pursued it with a passion. I've always been a driven person, and when I make up my mind to achieve something, I will work night and day to make it happen. I loved music and theater and before I finished high school I was doing some professional acting, performing almost continuously, and getting ready to go to college in Michigan to study piano performance and vocal performance.

Some people have a testimony about meeting God because they were broken and in despair. My story isn't like that. I met the Lord because I got everything I wanted and life was still empty. College was going really well. I was on a full scholarship, acting in the theater, and playing and singing in concerts and recitals. I won competitions and parts in plays, I got straight A's, and I had friends and a cute boyfriend. But I would go home at night and know that my relationships were shallow, and that no one really had the answers or cared much about me after the stage lights went down. There had to be more to life than this.

I started to really think about happiness. Did I know anyone who was truly happy? Did I know anyone who seemed to have that secret to life? The answer was yes. I knew a couple, and they were my parents.

Growing up, my parents worked for Young Life, a Christian organization that reaches out to high school students through clubs and summer camps. Young Life was so much fun, and I loved being a kid in that environment, but it wasn't a job that people saw as successful. My dad was paid if there was money, but that wasn't all the time. My mom stayed home with us. Every piece of clothing we had was a hand-me-down or from the thrift shop, and it was just a given that there was never any extra money. We had what we needed but nothing more, and the definition of need was pretty strict. Then Dad went to law school when I was in grade school, and there were a lot of student loans. My parents weren't glamorous or rich, and they didn't have the toys I thought meant that you had made it, and yet they were totally happy. They loved each other, and they loved us. And I knew they would both say that the secret to their joy was that they both knew and loved Jesus.

The Bible says, "Train a child in the way he should go, and when he is old he will not turn from it" (Proverbs 22:6). My parents had not only told me about their faith, but they had lived it out in our home for my entire life. I thank God for them and for their witness. After five years of trying to do it my way, I decided to turn back to God.

Jennifer's parents, Dave and Beth Chilcoat

The Bible teaches that everyone has done things that are contrary to God's will, and that we are all imperfect (Romans 3:23). Our sins are what separate us from God, who is perfect, and the penalty for sin is death (Romans 6:23). But when Jesus came to earth, He did not sin, and so He did not have to die. He chose to die anyway, and sacrificed Himself as a substitute for us. He paid off the debt of sin that we owe and all we have to do is accept His gift. If we acknowledge Jesus as our Lord and believe that God raised Him from the dead, we are saved from our sins and can live with God forever (Romans 10:9-10).

I wanted that. I had seen firsthand how a relationship with God had changed my parents' lives completely, and I wanted the peace and happiness that I saw in them. I prayed, "Okay, God, I want to try it Your way. Please forgive me and lead my life now. And if all this is true, please change my heart and help me want to follow You." It was my sophomore year in college.

Up until that time, I hadn't known many Christians my age. The few I knew weren't close friends. Soon after I made this commitment to God, I realized I was going to have to find some Christian friends to help support my decision or I was never going to stick with it. There was a guy I knew from my college choir who was a strong Christian. I asked him where he went to church and he took me with him that Sunday. We ended up getting married after graduation, and Nathan is still one of the best blessings and best Christian friends I have ever had.

Nathan and I moved to New York for graduate school after college. He was working on his doctorate in physics at Stony Brook on Long Island while I completed my master's at The Manhattan School of Music for vocal performance. I studied opera and classical voice and performed quite a bit in New York.

My goal was to be a professor of music. After my graduation, Nathan still had two years to go on his doctorate. I intended to get a doctorate as well, but it was hard to face more tuition while he was still in school. We thought it might be a good time to have a baby since it would be impossible to do that while in school for voice. Most classical singers take a complete professional hiatus when they are expecting because it's impossible to breathe around a baby in the way classical singing requires, and the hormones change your voice while you are pregnant. We were thinking Nathan could finish up while we started our family and then I would have the freedom to go wherever I wanted for my doctorate.

Now that I'm a mom, I laugh when I remember how easy I thought it would be to have a baby and do a doctorate. Of course! It's that simple! As soon as we had our first child, I was so in love with her, I didn't know how I would ever dedicate the amount of time needed for a doctorate and be away from home for the classes. Besides, a baby was a lot of work! I know a lot of women have done it, but I'm not sure I could have managed. God had others plans for me anyway, but it would take a while for me to see that. Our daughter was born in New York, and we named her Rinnah which means "song of joy."

During those two years before Nathan's graduation, we became involved in the high school ministry at our church. Having grown up in Young Life, I knew what effective youth ministry looked like, and this wasn't it. I didn't really want to be involved in youth ministry, but I thought, "They really need something else. They need Young Life."

Feeling helpful, I called Young Life and asked where their nearest ministry was, thinking that we could maybe connect our youth to that. I was told that they were just starting the ministry in the New York City area, the closest one was an hour away, and they were looking for staff in our area. I thought, "Um, no thank you. I am a singer." But still, I called the area director hoping we might be able to take our kids to a Young Life camp that summer.

Almost before I knew it we had a couple of vans full of kids headed to Virginia. I watched these New York kids who were savvy and tough and never let people see what they were feeling respond to the truth of the Gospel. They had hope. They felt loved. There was such a transformation! It was a week I will never forget and before it ended I had an interview with the regional director under a ropes course, and agreed to be the area director for a new Young Life ministry in our part of Long Island.

My parents really didn't know what to think. My dad was happy that I was walking in his footsteps and working for this ministry that he loved so much, but I think they had been a little unsure about how devoted I was to my faith. My parents took this new job as an indicator that my relationship with God had grown. They knew my faith must have been sincere if I would take that step.

We partnered with our church, so I was both the Young Life area director and the youth leader at our church, and Nathan was as committed to it as his school schedule would allow. We threw ourselves into the ministry, and Rinnah spent most of her first year in a backpack going to Young Life kids' field hockey games and plays and walking around camps. She just thought the view over my shoulders was the norm, and she became almost an unofficial high school mascot.

I loved the ministry, I loved the Lord, and I loved what I saw Him doing through Nathan and me. And yet, it was still a disorienting time. I had been single-minded my whole life about what I wanted, and it had not been youth ministry. It was music. I had practiced forty hours a week since I left for college, taken 130 college music class credit hours, and completed a two year master's program in music. My entire identity was music. Now, when people asked me what I did, I had no idea how to answer. I literally couldn't choke out the words, "I'm in youth ministry," because I was a musician! Wasn't I? Who was I if I wasn't a full-time musician?

God really used this time to show me a lot about yielding and my true identity. I had to come to terms with the fact that I wasn't in control of my life, and that my identity wasn't about what I did. I was not a musician, but a child of God. I was good at music, but that was a gift He'd given me, and it was one that was meant to be used for His purpose and His glory, not my own. God loved that I loved music, but He wanted me to love Him more.

God was so faithful to us in that period of our lives. There was never a time I didn't feel He was with me, and my faith was growing. We watched God provide everything we needed, not only financially as poor graduate students, but also as new parents, and as people new to the ministry. I began to accept that His will for me was good and perfect, even if it was not what I was expecting. I knew that we could trust Him even when we had no idea what He was doing. And, most importantly, I now knew my identity. It wasn't that I was in youth ministry or that I was a musician or that I was a mom or a wife. Those were things I did, but they were not who I was. I was a Christ-follower and a child of God. And knowing that made me better at everything else.

I also found a new respect and love for my family and my upbringing. I never knew until our experience in ministry in New York how uncommon it was to have an intact family who loved each other. I used to think broken homes were the exception, but now that I had contact with so many kids and so many families, I understood that broken homes were more the rule, and we were the exception. I really cherished my family back in Ohio, and missed them a lot while we were on the East Coast. There was so much I loved about New York, but it was not home.

God knew that I needed to learn to trust Him. I needed to know that my life belonged to Him and that He was faithful. God also knew that I needed to know who was in charge and who I was in this world. After I learned those lessons of trust, identity, and yielding, God let me go back to music, and He led me back home.

CHAPTER 3

Back to Ohio

When Rinnah was almost one, Nathan finished his doctorate, and we felt God calling us to move back to my hometown, Columbus, Ohio. I started teaching voice at Cedarville University and singing with the Columbus Symphony. I missed my Young Life kids a lot, but I was so happy to be back in music and I was thrilled to have realized my dream of being a college professor without having to do a doctorate. I was also offered a part-time job as the worship and music director at a church. Nathan started working as a research scientist, and then switched fairly quickly to computer programming. He found a good job working only a few miles from our house. Everything was moving along beautifully.

In the new church job, the pastor asked me to transition the service from traditional hymns to a mixed format including traditional music and contemporary worship music. They wanted me to start a worship band. I told them I would be terrible at that since I was an opera singer, and no one wants to hear an opera singer in a worship band! They asked me to pray about it and told me they thought I was the person God had sent to their church.

I did pray about it, and felt I was supposed to do the job, but I was really out of my comfort zone. I knew nothing about technology, sound systems, that style of singing, or lead sheets. It was a lot to take in and I was really afraid I would look stupid! My ability to lead a band improved, but I worried about what this style of singing was doing to my classical voice. Here I was a voice professor, and I was singing in a way that I would have counseled any of my students to avoid. Classical vocal technique is very sensitive and if one sings in other ways, it can make it difficult to go back.

About a year later, I braved teaching while I was pregnant again, and we had our second daughter, Rachel. Our life just seemed charmed. The girls brought such joy to our lives, and being a mom was wonderful. However, it was hard to balance mothering with my job expectations, and I wanted more time with the girls. I asked God to let me out of my church job but felt He was calling me to give up the symphony instead. What? I couldn't believe it. This was what I had worked toward for my entire career! After a hard struggle with myself over whether or not to obey God in this area, I did quit the symphony, but it didn't make much sense to me at the time.

I had started writing music for the worship band at church, just a few songs here and there. I wanted to express what God was teaching me in my own quiet times, and songwriting was a great new medium. I also set scripture verses to music and used them in the services at my church. But while I was finding more joy in contemporary worship music, I still didn't know why God was keeping me in my church position when I was trained in classical music. It just didn't fit with my goals! Feeling stretched for time, I asked God again if I could leave the church job, but I never sensed that was His direction for me, so I stayed.

Other than the press for time, our life seemed nearly perfect. Nathan had a good job, our kids were beautiful and so much fun for us, I loved teaching at the university and the church job was going well in spite of my reservations. We were in a comfortable house just down the street from my parents. We were so much closer to both of our families that we were able to see them frequently and our kids were growing up with their cousins. We felt blessed.

We decided we'd like to have another baby. With the girls, it had happened quickly, but this time something was different. We weren't getting pregnant, and as the months went on, I began to understand some of the heartbreak of my friends who had trouble conceiving. After a year, we were planning a trip to Hilton Head, South Carolina, with the girls, and I found out I was pregnant just before we left. We were so elated! I hoped my morning sickness wouldn't ruin our vacation, but even that seemed to go better than we expected. I had been terribly sick with the girls, but this time I wasn't sick at all. What a wonderful surprise! I was nearly twelve weeks pregnant, and we decided to tell our families when we got home. Both of Nathan's sisters-in-law were expecting and we would have three cousins all born within weeks of each other. How fun!

We went to Hilton Head and had a fabulous week playing on the beach with the girls. Our last night, we went on a dolphin spotting cruise, and asked someone to take a picture of all of us in the back of the boat. We were leaving in the morning, and I wanted to remember how happy we were with our beautiful family, knowing we had another child coming and that life was good. Still to this day I label that picture in my head with the caption "When We Were Happy," because everything changed the next day.

We left early the next morning to drive the twelve hours home. I wanted to make it back in one day so that I would not miss Sunday morning services. I was experiencing an unusual pain off and on in my shoulder, so I tried to move around as much as possible. As the day went on, the pain became increasingly worse, and I thought I must have pulled a muscle. We made it home in very good time and got in early that evening. Nathan told me to go lie down while he put the girls to bed.

I laid down but I couldn't get comfortable. Around midnight, I was really struggling to breathe, but I didn't know who to call to watch the girls so we could go get help. I don't remember why, but every member of my immediate family was out of town that night and I didn't want to wake a neighbor. Then we made one of the less intelligent decisions of our lives. I told Nathan I would be fine and we should just go to sleep. If I still couldn't breathe in the morning, then we would go to the hospital. He still says that is the last time he will listen to me in medical matters!

The "When We Were Happy" picture

When Nathan woke me up in the morning, I could hardly move. I was in intense pain, and I was still having difficulty breathing. We got someone to come and watch our girls and Nathan drove me to the hospital. We had to call the church and tell them I wouldn't be there that morning. I said to Nathan in the car, "Well, at least we know this can't be an ectopic pregnancy or something because I'm already twelve weeks. We would know by now, wouldn't we?"

When we got to the hospital, everything moved quickly. I don't remember a lot of it, but I do remember the doctor coming in and saying, "Jennifer, this is just not a viable pregnancy." I asked her what she meant and she said, "We cannot save this pregnancy."

I didn't know why she would say something so unreasonable. Of course they would help my baby! I said, "But, my baby, you need to help my baby, I don't understand."

She replied, "This was an ectopic pregnancy. Your tube has burst. You are bleeding internally and we must get you into surgery right now." She said it gently, but each word felt like a physical blow.

We didn't realize how serious the situation was. Afterward, I was told I had lost over 30% of my blood due to internal hemorrhaging and could have died. My difficulty breathing the night before had been because I was going into shock. That would also explain my poor decision making that night! The hemorrhaging had inexplicably slowed while I was sleeping, which was the only reason I didn't bleed out. The doctor told me they didn't understand why the bleeding had stopped since that does not normally happen.

I was absolutely devastated. I had never dealt with loss or pain of this magnitude, and I just didn't know what to do with it. I was also panicking about the fact that I could have just left my girls without a mother. Suddenly nothing seemed safe. I didn't even want Nathan to leave the house. I was terrified that something would happen to one of us! I felt so physically weak from the loss of blood, and I was totally grief stricken over losing this baby that we had wanted so much.

Our loss was also very public. Because we'd gone to the hospital on a Sunday morning, the entire church knew there had been an emergency, and everyone wanted to know if I was okay and what happened. I hated having to tell everyone. I knew they loved me, and people could not have been more kind, but emotionally I was so raw that even their glances hurt me. It was so personal, and I would have chosen to keep it private.

That was one of the first times, though, that I really saw Romans 8:28 come to life. God promises in that verse that He will use all things for good for those who love the Lord. After I lost the baby, people in my church talked to me in ways they never had before. There were women around me who were hurting, and apparently my life had looked too perfect. They never thought I would understand their situations. Now that I had experienced some pain and loss of my own, they opened up to me, and I found a new depth to my ministry and my friendships.

CHAPTER 4

A Shock

October 2003

It had been two months since my miscarriage and I was physically well enough to go back to my vocal teaching at the university. Those months were difficult emotionally. In addition to recovering from the loss of our baby, my beloved great-aunt, Midge, had passed away and I was also worried about my dad. He wasn't feeling well and we didn't know why.

My father was the best dad ever and absolutely foundational in my life. If there was anything I didn't know, I could count on Dad to know it. If anyone ever needed help with anything at anytime, Dad would be there to help. He was awesome and hilarious and brilliant and I loved him tremendously. He was also an athlete and a very strong man. He'd been lifting weights at the gym (a practice I've never adopted!) and thought he had pulled a muscle. It wasn't healing so he was having some testing done.

After a while it became clear that a muscle pull wasn't all it was, but we weren't too worried. Dad had always been so healthy that he rarely even caught a cold. We were waiting for the test results when I received an email between students at the university just a few weeks after going back. It said that Dad had been diagnosed with amyotrophic lateral sclerosis (ALS), also known as Lou Gehrig's disease.

Dave Chilcoat

I had no idea what ALS was, so I googled it to find out what we would do about it. I assumed there would be a treatment plan, or some expectation of how long it would take Dad to recover. The very first words I saw on the screen were: "Fatal." "No treatment." "No cure." "Average life expectancy of eighteen months to three years."

I was absolutely stunned. I sat there staring at the screen. I simply couldn't comprehend those words. Then the reality of it broke over me and I began to sob in my office.

I don't even remember driving home, but I went straight to my parents' house, and found what felt like a million people already there. Dad was loved by everyone who met him and he seemed to know the whole world. It was a joke in our family that he never went anywhere without running into people he knew. Once we lost Dad at Disney World, and when we finally found him again, he was chatting with an old friend from Pittsburgh.

I couldn't tell you who else was at my parents' house, though, because I only saw my dad. There he was, smiling and trying to cheer people up. He looked at me with such love and sadness because he knew his diagnosis was causing *me* pain! He just reached out to hug me. It was so like him to try to comfort all of us rather than be comforted.

I went home that night and fell asleep. When I woke up, I had forgotten Dad's diagnosis for the moment. Everything felt normal. Then I remembered and it was like hitting a wall of pain. I couldn't even catch my breath because it hurt so badly. Nathan had already gone to work and Rinnah and Rachel were still asleep. I remember thinking, "Wake up, wake up! I need something to do! I need something to take my mind off this terrible pain. Please!" The girls had never slept late in their lives and I had already learned that when things that never happen do happen, I should pay attention. It occurred to me in that moment that God was giving me time with Him.

I went downstairs and knelt by my couch to pray, but I couldn't even form the words. I just lay down on the floor, crying, and opened my Bible at random. The very first thing I saw there leapt off the page. It was as if the words of Psalm 42 were highlighted just for me. "Why are you downcast, O my soul? Why so disturbed within me? Put your hope in God, for I will yet praise him, my Savior and my God."

I stopped crying and sat up. I knew that the Lord was speaking to me, and I was astonished that He was being so direct and personal. "Lord," I prayed, "I don't have any hope. They have told us there is none, so how can I put my hope in You? But if You give me some hope, I will put it in You."

I turned the page and immediately saw Psalm 46. "God is our refuge and strength, an ever-present help in trouble. Therefore we will not fear, though the earth give way and the mountains fall into the heart of the sea, though its waters roar and foam and the mountains quake with their surging... 'Be still, and know that I am God; I will be exalted among the nations, I will be exalted in the earth.' The Lord Almighty is with us; the God of Jacob is our fortress."

Right there I knew what God was telling me. God was bigger than any of these troubles. God is God. I was to trust Him and see what He would do. He always knows the bigger picture that we can't see, and even when we are going through things we would never choose, we can trust the character of God. We can trust His promises. I felt as shaken as if the mountains were falling into the sea, but God was bigger. God would be my fortress. God would be my parents' fortress. And God would protect us. And somehow, through all of this, we would praise the name of the Lord.

I went to my piano and from those verses wrote a song called "Be Still":

Why are you downcast, my soul, my soul?
Why so discouraged within me?
Put all your hope in the Lord, my soul.
He'll have the glory, He'll have the victory.

And I know I yet will praise my God.
He yet will deliver me.
So do not fear, though the mountains may tremble
And the earth pass away,
Though the mountains may fall into the sea.

Be still and know He is God, my soul.
You can depend on His sovereignty.
Just rest yourself in the Lord, my soul.
He'll be exalted through all eternity.

And I know I yet will praise my God.
He yet will deliver me.
So do not fear, though the mountains may tremble
And the earth pass away,
Though the mountains may fall into the sea.

Be still, and know that I am God.
Be still, and know that I am God.
I will be exalted among the nations of the earth.
I will be exalted in your life from your new birth.
Be still.

Later I went and played the song for my parents. My dad had always been proud of anything I did. His parents had not been involved in his activities, so he was always determined to support us in everything we tried. It wasn't always easy for this guy who loved everything about sports and didn't have an artistic bone in his body to get excited about watching his daughter's latest recital or theater performance, yet he was always there in the audience, smiling at me with such pride in his eyes.

He loved this song and my mom did, too. Dad said what he liked most about it was the way it reminded him of God's Word and God's promises. I didn't realize it then, but God was starting something new with that song; something that would eventually begin an entirely new ministry and life for us. At that moment, I was just glad that the song reminded my dad and my family that God was still in control.

CHAPTER 5

Welcome, Toby!

January 2004

After several months, we were told it was safe to try to get pregnant again. I was scared this time. It had never really occurred to me that being pregnant could be dangerous in the modern age, but now I knew differently. My chances of another ectopic pregnancy were greater now, and my chances of getting pregnant had gone down. I wasn't sure if I was ready to go through all the emotion of trying again, but we really wanted a third child.

Imagine our joy when I became pregnant almost right away! I was also happy that it had happened so quickly because Dad was already deteriorating, and it was very important to me that he get to know his new grandchild. My morning sickness returned in full force, which I took as a positive sign, and at our first appointment, the doctors told us this would be a normal pregnancy.

The pregnancy went fine for the first two trimesters, and we were delighted to discover we were having a boy. This would be the first grandson after seven granddaughters for my parents. Rinnah and Rachel were so excited to be getting their very own baby! Rinnah would be able to talk about him at show-and-tell in kindergarten while Rachel could help me with him at home. They were ecstatic! They helped me get his room ready and patted my stomach a lot. Since he was due in October, I arranged to take the fall semester off from the university to get our family settled and made plans to go back to teaching in January.

At about twenty-nine weeks, I went into labor for the first time. Rinnah was born a couple weeks before her due date, and Rachel had arrived almost a month early, but I'd never had anything like this. We went to the hospital and they were able to stop the contractions after about twelve hours of labor. The doctor put me on bed rest and I went home to wait.

Over the next few weeks, I had several more bouts of labor, including one very serious incident where I was hospitalized for a few days. The doctors put me on a medication to stop the labor which suppressed my neurological system so much that they had to stop administering it. It was during the Olympics, which is about the only sporting event I truly love, and I remember lying in my hospital bed watching the swimming races. I wondered when they had changed all the rules since the swimmers seemed to be switching lanes at random and even the lane markers were moving by themselves. Then my doctor came in and, speaking very slowly, told me I wasn't responding well to the drugs. I guess not! I was very concerned about what this could be doing to the baby, but they said that the possible side effects from the medication were still far better than delivering him more than two months early.

The doctors finally got the labor stopped and I went home again. I made it to thirty-six weeks and they let me off bed rest, but after all those early labor experiences, our little boy waited another two weeks to be delivered! We named him Tobias, which means "God is good." We called him Toby for short, and were so incredibly relieved to see that he was perfectly healthy. Later, my doctor told us that given the last two pregnancies, it would be too dangerous for me to get pregnant again, so we were doubly grateful for the safe arrival of Toby.

My whole family visited us in the hospital. At this point, Dad was still walking fine with a little help from a cane, and with my parents and all my brothers and their families, it was a very full hospital room. My parents gave Toby a present and the accompanying card read, "Dear

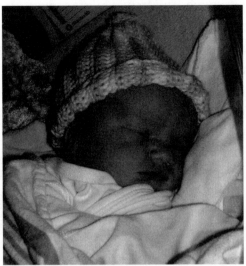

Toby, at last

Toby, we are so excited that God has blessed us by lending you to us. We can't wait to see the enormous plans and wonderful blessings He has for your life as He begins and completes a good work in you. We love you!" Who would have dreamed that God's plans and blessings for our little guy would start with such a difficult path?

From the beginning, Toby was a pretty challenging baby. He was fussy and he didn't sleep well. The girls were both sleeping through the night at eight or nine weeks of age, but Toby didn't sleep through the night until he was well over six months old, and that was with me doing everything I knew to make that happen. It seemed strange to me because for some reason I knew he wanted to be much more easy-going than he was.

Toby did fine when he was with me or Nathan, but he would rarely let anyone else touch him, including my parents. We couldn't leave him in the nursery at church or with a sitter. Other than that and his difficulty sleeping, he seemed to be doing well for his first six months. He loved his sisters and would babble and make faces and play with them for hours. We thought he was just perfect. We chalked up his shyness with others to intense separation anxiety or perhaps a personality trait.

Raising three young children while keeping up with my church worship job was catching up with me, though. It was so much harder because we weren't sleeping and Toby needed a lot of attention. I spoke with the department chair at the university and he said they could manage without me for the next semester since they had hired someone new when I'd left in the fall. This let me extend my sabbatical, and I was grateful for the extra time at home.

Rachel and Rinnah were always great sisters to Toby

I remember being a little intimidated by having a boy after two girls. So many people said, "Oh, just wait, you're in for it now! Your house is going to be a wreck! You're always going to be pulling him out of things and off things. It's going to be so different!" It made me nervous, but to our surprise, Toby was actually our most passive baby. Our daughter, Rachel, was a stunt baby by comparison! For example, Toby loved television, which I thought was odd since the girls had never liked TV until they were well past twelve months old. He wanted to be held all the time, but if there was something to watch, sometimes he would let us put him down. He didn't move much, though. He would just lie there and observe whatever was happening around him.

Things started to go downhill after the first six months. Toby was suffering from repeated ear infections which were so frequent that he rarely had one clear up before another began. He was in a lot of pain, and he became more demanding and less able to cope with any change. We could never put him down, and we couldn't leave him for any amount of time. He cried a lot. It was exhausting. It became clear that we would never be able to leave him with someone else, so I finally called the university and told them I would not be coming back. It was a blow. I had always wanted to be a professor of music, and I really loved teaching, but my kids had to be my priority at that time and it was the only thing to do.

We were concerned about Toby's hearing as well. His ears drums had burst repeatedly due to the severity of his ear infections, and that kind of damage can cause hearing loss. The pediatrician and the ear, nose, and throat specialist finally agreed on surgery to insert tubes in Toby's ears when he was a year old. The tubes helped a little, but they kept getting blocked and the ear infections continued.

In spite of the pain from his constant ear infections, though, Toby was a sweet little guy. He loved us and wanted to be with us. He had some unusual habits which made us laugh. For instance, he would never let us pull his shirt sleeves up if he seemed to be too warm. If my sleeves were pushed up on my arms, he would point at them and look so concerned that I would let him pull them down. He would do this with such a serious expression on his face. Then he would look up and smile at me as if to say, "There, you must feel so much better!" We just accepted that he was a quirky guy. After all, when our oldest daughter was a toddler, she had spent six months greeting water towers whenever she was in the car. We thought Toby must just have a thing about sleeves!

Toby reached many of his milestones late, but we weren't too worried. Both of the girls had crawled and walked later than average, and we figured it ran in the family. Toby did a strange military crawl, dragging himself along the floor with his arms, until well after his first birthday, and he didn't really walk until he was sixteen months old. We still thought he would catch up.

Toby doing his military crawl at eleven months

We were getting concerned about his speech, though. Both our girls had walked late and talked early, but Toby was still just babbling. We took him in for a complete hearing screening when he was about twelve months old. His hearing was tested for the softest sounds he could distinguish at many different pitch ranges. Being able to hear sounds under twenty decibels is considered normal, and numbers over twenty-five are considered hearing impaired. Toby kept coming in at twenty-three to twenty-five. For comparison, we were told that most children test between five and ten. These results put him in the borderline hearing impaired range. They used the term "clinically deaf" to describe it, meaning that his ears had been so full of fluid for so long that he hadn't been able to hear. He also had some extensive scarring and damage to his ear drums from all the ear infections, and they didn't think the scarring was likely to improve.

This was hard news to receive. We didn't want Toby to deal with hearing impairment for the rest of his life. He was still getting ear infections and I was worried that the situation would continue to deteriorate. It was good to have some explanation for his slow speech, but I wasn't sure I totally accepted that as the reason.

When Rinnah was little, we always used to laugh about the fact that she talked so loudly. We found out when she was three or four years old that she needed tubes in her ears and after the surgery she immediately began speaking more quietly. We felt so badly that we had teased her about it when, in reality, she just couldn't hear well! However, her poor hearing hadn't stopped her from learning to speak. She had actually learned to talk earlier than average. Why would Toby's hearing issues prevent him from developing speech if they weren't bad enough to fall into the category of true hearing impairment?

Toby had a second surgery to correct the ear tubes and remove his adenoids, and that seemed to really help. His ear infections stopped, and we relaxed a little. At least it didn't appear that his hearing was going to get worse. His screening numbers dropped to about twenty-one, and we were told that would probably be as good as it would get due to all of the scarring. The improvement was enough, however, that Toby did not need hearing aids and we were thankful.

CHAPTER 6

A New Musical Endeavor

Fall 2005

I t was at about this time that I started making my first album. My dad had always supported everything I did, but I knew that my classical singing wasn't really his cup of tea. He absolutely loved the music I wrote and played with the worship band at church, so I decided to record an album of the songs I had been writing, including "Be Still," for his Christmas present.

I really had no idea what I was doing. It was pretty intimidating to search for a studio and producer, and though I had done recordings before, they were all classical, which is a completely different process. I didn't want to make an expensive mistake, and I didn't want to come out looking (or sounding!) foolish. I knew I couldn't afford a big studio in Nashville or New York. It wouldn't have mattered even if I could because I couldn't leave the kids or my dad long enough to record an album away from home.

After some research, I decided I was looking for someone who had produced a number of independent projects and who worked locally in Columbus. I also knew that I needed a very specific skill set on a contemporary album, and someone who knew what they were doing with this genre. As a classical singer, I needed a producer I could trust to take my music and my voice and make me sound believable in a contemporary band.

I just kept coming back to the same website – Workbook Studio. They had an incredible list of albums to their credit, and they were right in downtown Columbus. I decided to call the studio, and when I looked up their phone number, the contact name was Jon Chinn. I did a double take. I had gone to high school with a Jon Chinn who was a couple years ahead of me in school. We'd had a few friends in common and I'd even been to some cast parties for school plays at his house. I didn't think it could be the same guy, but then I looked through the website and saw that his business partner was Neil Schmitt. I knew Neil Schmitt too – he was the drummer for Jon's high school band that I had thought was so cool. My best friend at the time had dated the bass player in their group.

Well, now I didn't think I could call Workbook Studio after all. I really didn't know how people who knew me in high school would react to me as a Christian artist. It was embarrassing. I didn't want to look like a hypocrite. I had no idea what Jon and Neil might believe at this point either, and wondered if they would even be open to producing a Christian album.

I prayed about it a lot, and decided that I should at least call them. The worst case scenario was that they would say no and I would feel dumb. And let's face it, in the arts, if you're not willing to take risks and look stupid sometimes, you'll never get anything done. And maybe, rather than a hypocrite, they would see someone whose life was changed by Christ.

I called Jon and we had a great talk. He was very open to helping me out. He invited me down to see the studio and to talk through my project. When I got there, it was in a pretty rough neighborhood, and Jon came out to let me in and escort me up. It was an old warehouse space that they had renovated. The other tenants were all visual artists because "painting is quiet." There was art everywhere and the atmosphere was amazing, but none of that could hide the fact that this was not a high-end studio. The heat didn't always work. A lot of windows were broken. I wouldn't feel comfortable walking out to my car alone at night.

Jon was obviously a lover of sound, though. He collected amazing old gear, instruments, microphones and amplifiers, and he used them all for whatever unique effect he could achieve with them. He taught me so much about how to listen and create contemporary sound in a recording which was totally different than the techniques I had used to produce live, acoustic, classical sound.

Jon Chinn at Workbook Studio

When I left that day, we agreed to work together and, looking back, I really have to laugh at myself. I was thinking that it looked like he knew what he was doing but he could probably use the work. I would do him a favor! I didn't know that he had songs on the radio all over the country, on television and in movies. Jon was quite highly regarded. I thought I was helping him out, but in actuality, he was squeezing me in just because he'd known me in high school and felt badly that my dad was dying.

I told Jon that this was the most expensive gift I had ever contemplated giving to anyone. Our budget was extremely low for an album, but it was still a lot of money for us. When we talked about quality, I asked him to help me produce the project as cheaply as possible without it being embarrassing. How's that for setting the bar low?

Working on that album was simultaneously completely frustrating and amazingly fun. I hate feeling stupid, and I felt stupid a lot. I had learned a good bit of technology for live contemporary sound at the church, but for a girl who had never done anything but classical music until a few years before, this was a big leap. I was torn between the anxiety of never knowing what I was doing and the sheer joy of recording my own music. It was difficult, but it was also exhilarating!

I didn't understand half of what Jon was talking about and my areas of musical expertise weren't much help in this arena. He was extremely patient with me and I learned so much about recording this way. For example, contemporary vocal technique is completely different from classical, and the recording is so unforgiving, exposing every little problem. When I sang my way, it didn't work well with a microphone because that style of singing isn't meant to use one. I had to be willing to try new things and I couldn't stay in my comfort zone. I had to just jump in and be willing to fail sometimes.

We completed the recording in time to give the album to my dad for his Christmas present. The artwork wasn't done, though, so the actual album wasn't released until the following February. I say "released" tongue-in-cheek. Basically, that just meant we told people at our church that they could have a copy of the CD then. I wasn't trying to get the music out; I just wanted Dad to have it.

It was truly a home-grown project. My brother, Andy, played the bass and my uncle, Ed, played the guitar. The drummer from church, Sam, did the percussion and an old family friend, Ryan, did the backing vocals. Jon and I played everything else. My choir from church even came to the studio and recorded backing vocals on some of the pieces.

Imagine my surprise when the choir members and my parents' friends started talking about it, and we sold enough albums to pay for the project in only six weeks! It was unbelievable. We started to wonder if God was giving us a new ministry, but it seemed impossible to pursue with what we were going through at the time. Since we couldn't leave

Working on the album *Be Still*

Toby with other people and my mom and dad needed so much help, it was a huge sacrifice just to get me to the studio.

We had someone offer to list us on a service that sent singles to radio. The service was not going to promote anything, and radio programmers would literally have to stumble across my songs and choose to listen. It was about $30, and we were told to expect nothing. Radio promotion is a big business, and the chance of someone noticing my music, taking the time to listen, and then choosing to add an independently made "cheap but not embarrassing" song seemed ludicrous. Even so, we thought we'd take a chance for $30. Our church seemed to like it so much, and everyone kept telling us to try. We signed up that spring of 2006 and promptly forgot about it.

CHAPTER 7

Questions

Spring 2006

W e hoped that since Toby could hear better now, his speech would catch up, but it didn't. He was actually losing sounds. As a baby, Toby had started to babble normally, although later than average, and for a while it seemed like his speech would be fine. He gained a few sounds, and had a word or two, but then the words went away. Over time, I noticed even the sounds disappearing, and that really concerned me. He was communicating with his hands and facial expressions, but the only sounds he made were "bo" for wet things (water, the tub, his cup, the rain, the ocean) and "ma" which usually meant Nathan or I. I had heard that speech regression was a big marker for autism, and this set off alarm bells in my head. The pediatrician reassured us, though, and told us to wait a little longer – Toby was only eighteen months old and he'd had so many hearing problems. She said that if he still wasn't talking by age two we would look into it.

Another aspect that was really becoming a concern was Toby's eating. I had nursed Toby when he was a baby, which had gone fine, but he had never been interested in solid food. At first, we laughed at the terrible faces he made when eating, thinking he was just a funny baby, but it quickly stopped being humorous. I prided myself on having kids who would accept a variety of foods. At age three, Rachel told everyone that her favorite food was roasted red pepper hummus, and in kindergarten Rinnah adored Japanese food. We had always been very intentional about introducing many kinds of foods to our children. Toby had very few baby foods he would tolerate, and, rather than gaining more, he was actually losing foods he would willingly eat.

Since baby food was a failure, we tried to transition him to regular food. We thought that maybe it was a texture issue. He just wouldn't have it. The only things we could get him to eat were dry Cheerios, Rice Krispies, and prepackaged peanut butter crackers. If we changed the shape or brand of anything, he couldn't handle it. He would drink water or milk, and that was it. He had no fruits or vegetables or proteins. We were really concerned about his nutrition and, with our pediatrician's recommendation, we started him on supplements. We had to hold him and squirt them down the back of his throat. He was also anemic and had to have an iron supplement which was a terrible, thick, black liquid we'd have to get him to swallow.

It was such a hard time. My dad had grown significantly worse, and by this time was confined to a wheelchair and needed a lot of help. We were at my parents' house every day to give my mom a break and spend time with my dad. We were so sleep deprived. Even though Toby slept through the night most of the time at this point, all three of the kids were having a lot of nightmares, and it was always hard to get Toby back to sleep. Caring for Toby was just relentless because he wouldn't let anyone else touch him, not even for a minute. Getting a babysitter for a break was simply out of the question, and Toby was very hard to keep happy, even for us.

Some days were better than others. Sometimes Toby was happy to play at our local park on the climbing toys and swings and he would have a great time, laughing and climbing on things. I would think that everything was fine. Some days he wouldn't do it. He was usually happy at our neighborhood park, but he was afraid of unfamiliar parks. Some days, though, he was excited to try a new play area. It was very unpredictable. Often, when I parked the car to go somewhere, he would cry, but not always. I couldn't figure it out, and that uncertainty made everything stressful. Why was parking in the lot for the playground exciting one day and terrifying the next?

One of the stranger things was that Toby loved to swing upside down or be hugged really tightly, but he couldn't stand light touch of any kind. People at our church knew that Toby was shy with strangers, and often they would approach him gently and run their fingertips up his arm or ruffle his hair. He would inevitably cry and try to hide from them, which, of course, reinforced his reputation as a "tough baby." I got to the point that I felt I needed to tell people not to touch him at all, but how do you do that without offending people? And why was it that he couldn't stand a gentle caress, but he would belly laugh with delight when we threw him up in the air and caught him?

By the end of spring, Toby was about twenty months old and I was really getting concerned. He didn't play much at all, and he was only willing to touch things made of plastic or wood. He would get very upset if his hands were ever messy or got crumbs on them. We had a red chair in our family room that was Toby's favorite, and he would sit there all day. The only way to keep him happy was to let him sit in his chair and turn on the television. He never got down to play when we were home. I didn't know any other toddler who didn't play.

I felt like such a failure as a mom. I had never allowed the girls to watch much TV and I didn't want to use it to babysit Toby, but I didn't know what else to do. He was still not eating anything nutritious, and I was out of ideas. He was sad so often. We'd visit our extended families and the other babies his age were doing all kinds of things while mine just sat on my lap, not interacting except to wince or cry when anyone approached him. It was really hard to remember our life before Dad was sick and Toby needed so much attention.

It was very isolating. Here we were, absolutely in love with this baby, but knowing that he wasn't like the other kids. It was a constant fear in the back of my mind that there was something wrong. I just knew it. And it felt like we were the only ones who had a child like this. All the other babies we saw in our families and at church seemed to be developing right on target. We thought Toby was the most amazing baby in the whole world, but I worried that no one else would recognize how special and wonderful he was. Add to that the grief and sadness of knowing that we were going to lose Dad, and I felt completely alone, even in a room full of people. I wondered if anyone knew what was really happening in our family.

The "advice" we got from everyone was hard to take, too. Our immediate families were very supportive in general, but from others and often even strangers we got a lot of, "Are you going to let him get away with that?" "If you would just be firm with him, he wouldn't act that way." "Why don't you wait for him to get hungry? Then he'll eat." I sometimes just wanted to scream at people, "This is my kid! Don't you think we've thought about this more than you have? Don't you think we've looked for answers? Don't you think we've tried everything? Do you not see my two girls who eat everything and talk and play and interact? We're doing our best!" I knew that most of them were just

Touch the animals at the petting zoo? No.

trying to be helpful, but it wasn't. It made me feel even more alone and inadequate.

We were starting to see more worrisome behaviors. Toby began to be afraid to go outside and would get visibly upset at the sight of grass. He would only walk on hard surfaces, and he would only wear one pair of shoes. He had strong clothing preferences and would cry if we put a shirt on him with stitching or designs of any kind. He seemed really clumsy, and he fell a lot. He hit his head repeatedly, and I remember thinking that it was no wonder he didn't want to move around since he was always hurting himself when he did.

I could tell that Toby was really bright, though, and in some areas, he was brilliant. Someone had given us a huge box of wooden baby puzzles, and he loved them. He could do them all. I remember one day he was trying to get my attention. He would call out and then look toward whatever he wanted me to notice. This particular day he was sitting on the floor with the television on, and I was working in the adjacent kitchen, thinking he was just sitting there. He got my attention to show me what he'd done — there on the floor in front of my twenty-month-old baby was a completed forty piece floor puzzle belonging to his sister. It was stamped "Ages Six and Up" across the top.

I almost panicked. My first thought was the movie *Rain Man* and that Toby was a math savant. No twenty-month-old has that kind of spatial reasoning. It was frightening. I didn't know much about autism, but I had just started to consider that possibility and this seemed to be a confirmation. I had too many unanswered questions to think it was nothing. I ran to the phone and called my husband, and he tried to calm me down. He said, "Honey, I'm a nuclear physicist. Maybe he's just good at math." True. But it was still scary.

I know a lot more about autism now, but, at the time, all I knew of it was the most extreme end of the spectrum where children don't connect emotionally and may never communicate. I knew Toby was emotionally connected to us and loved us. He laughed with us and he made eye contact. He wanted to be involved, and he understood everything we said even if he couldn't talk back. He was pointing at things, and communicating with his body and facial expressions. I was starting to be sure there was something wrong, but I didn't think autism was it. It just didn't quite fit. I could talk myself out of really worrying about the possibility, but autism was always in the back of my mind.

It made me especially sad that Toby wouldn't allow my dad to hold him. All of our married siblings on both sides of our family had babies within a year of Toby's birth, so we had a lot of babies around for comparison. On my side, Toby's cousin, Kendal, was six weeks older and his cousin, Owen, was 3 months younger. At family gatherings, it was very obvious that the other babies were able to handle being held by different relatives and they were playful and social. Toby never was and I knew how much my dad wanted to be involved with him. It broke my heart. I wanted Toby to know and love his Papa so much, and our time was really limited. Why couldn't Toby let other people into his life?

Looking back, I think we would have pursued things with Toby earlier if it hadn't been for Dad's situation. Dad was declining more rapidly now and was having trouble with his breathing. At the end of the spring, he told us that he didn't think he would make it to his fifty-ninth birthday, which was in September of that year. I couldn't believe that would be true, but he seemed so sure. I knew he was deteriorating, but he seemed a long way from dying.

We were also misled because of Toby's hearing. Because he had such struggles in that area, it was easy to believe that Toby's speech delay would catch up on its own once he could hear again. Our pediatrician kept telling us not to worry yet, and, frankly, we didn't have time to pursue help so it was a relief to just think, "Okay, I must be overreacting. I can visit this again in six months, and it's probably fine anyway. Just deal with the most pressing thing right now." Besides, we really had no idea what the problem might be, so that made finding a solution seem that much more overwhelming. Where would we even start?

The other factor to our waiting was that there were many times when Toby seemed happy and fine. Of course, those were also the times when we had met very specific conditions – when Toby was with Nathan or me, when he was not eating, and wearing the right clothes, and not dirty, and so on – but he was still our sweet boy. He could have so much fun when he was just with his family. He was quirky, yes, but he was clearly intelligent and loving. The rest of it was just a mystery.

In perfect hindsight, I wish we'd listened to our instincts about Toby and at least had him tested earlier. We understand now how very important early intervention is for all special needs, and especially intervention before age three. The clock was already ticking and the advice to wait is widespread. Studies show that parents usually suspect a problem with their children six months to a year before professionals suggest testing just because parents know their children best. But we chose to wait it out. That was the advice we'd been given and we still hoped Toby might grow out of it. Besides, Dad needed all the help we could give right then.

CHAPTER 8

A God Appointment
June 2006

W e started what I've come to think of as "the last summer." Dad was dying. Before, there had always been a steady, slow worsening of symptoms. In June, though, it was as if he fell off a cliff. Very quickly he went from his wheelchair to his bed. He could no longer help himself in any way. His speech was labored because he had such a hard time breathing and then forcing the air out to talk. He couldn't use his hands at all, or turn himself in bed. If there was a position in which he couldn't breathe, he couldn't shift out of it or even get air in to tell us to move him. It was very frightening.

Dad needed help around the clock. I started scheduling people to come at night so my mom could get some rest. It wasn't hard. Dad had touched so many lives during his life that there was a waiting list of men from our church and community who wanted to come and help him, even though that usually meant they would have to stay up all night only to turn around the next morning and go to work with no sleep. I later heard from so many of them that it was one of the most memorable nights of their life because Dad really couldn't sleep and he would talk to them about God and about what he had learned because of his disease.

Dad had been blogging for almost his entire illness about what God was teaching him. What had started out as a website to save my parents time by quickly updating family and friends on Dad's condition had become an incredible tool for the Lord. Dad would write every week and every week people would log on from all over the world to find out what he said. He was very real in his journal, sometimes hilarious, sometimes heartbreaking, but always knowing with such certainty that God loved him and knew what was best. He wanted people to know that they could trust the character of God in any situation they faced.

So many people were touched by the journal, but it was getting harder and harder for Dad to write now. He had switched to voice-activated software when his hands stopped working, but he didn't even have the energy for that anymore. He wrote a few times in June. My mom wrote when he couldn't. He had to take so much morphine for the pain that the line between being asleep and being awake started to blur. It was hard for him to do anything for more than a few minutes because any effort was completely exhausting.

One of my favorite memories from that summer was his tenderness with the kids. There were nine grandchildren by this time and Dad loved nothing more than being with them. They would come and play games with him or just talk. My parents had added on a handicap accessible sun room when Dad was first diagnosed, and it had become his bedroom. We all spent hours in his room, especially the kids. There's something irresistible to children about knowing they are completely loved.

Our oldest, Rinnah, particularly loved to be with her Papa. She was seven years old that summer, and she would hang out in his sun room and talk to him and play games with him. She'd had a very scary start to the summer when she got a rare infection resulting in severe vertigo. She'd spent a week in the hospital while the doctors figured it out and administered heavy doses of antibiotics. After she came home, she spent even more time with my dad. I think being in the hospital had given her a greater appreciation for how he felt being stuck in bed. They had always played games together, and when his hands stopped working, Dad told Rinnah he wanted to teach her dominoes. She would stand his tiles up so he could see them, and he would tell her which ones to play for him. It was so like him to just quietly find a way around the difficulty and keep going.

At the end of June, Rinnah and Rachel started taking swimming lessons. We would go to the pool every morning and then drive over to my parents' house for the afternoon. Then we would head home again for dinner, put the kids to bed, and often Nathan or I would go back to my mom and dad's in the evening to help.

Toby didn't like being at the pool. He didn't want his feet to touch the wet pool decking and he didn't want to be anywhere near the water. If he got a drop of water on him, he would cry instantly, almost as though he was being burned. We didn't understand it, but we knew to avoid it at all costs. It was just easier to carry him the whole time and Toby and I would sit well away from the edge of the pool so he wouldn't get splashed as we watched his sisters' lessons. Looking back, I am amazed at how many things I did for him unconsciously, not realizing the number of adjustments I made for him.

One day as we were leaving the pool, I ran into an acquaintance from high school. I stood there holding Toby while Rinnah and Rachel sat talking together and her two boys ran around. She asked about my family. I told her about Dad, so the conversation took a little longer than it normally would have.

As we talked, I noticed that she frequently corrected her older son, but didn't seem to notice the behavior of her younger boy much, even though, to my mind, it was quite a bit worse. He was randomly wandering around and running into things and shouting when she was talking and just being generally disruptive. I thought it was really strange, and somewhat unfair to her older child. Then she said, "Well, it has been difficult, but now that we have the autism diagnosis, at least we know what we're dealing with." When I realized that her son was autistic, suddenly his behavior and hers made a lot more sense.

I decided to just test the water. "I didn't realize your son was autistic. How did you know? Because, well, Toby doesn't talk."

"How old is he?" she asked.

"He's twenty-one months. He started to talk, but then he stopped and he's lost those words. He understands us, and follows directions and everything, but he doesn't talk."

"Yeah, that's concerning. Have you talked to your pediatrician?"

"Yes. She told us to wait until he's two and see if he catches up."

"That's what they usually say. The problem with that is if you wait until the fall, he'll never get into the programs. You might not be able to get him in now."

I didn't know what she was talking about. "What programs?" I asked.

"The early intervention programs. You really need to call Help Me Grow."

I didn't realize it then, but that conversation was a God appointment. I had never heard of Help Me Grow, but it was the local name of the federal program for children with special needs under the age of three. It has different names all over the country, which is confusing, but since the program is federal, it is available in every county in the United States.

She told me that Help Me Grow would come out for free and test Toby for developmental delays and tell me what kind of help he might need. They also provide special needs services if you qualify, which meant that we might be able to get free therapy if there was an issue. Many of the programs in our area, though, ran on the school calendar, and since it was already June and we hadn't even started the testing process, we weren't likely to get a spot in one of the better programs.

As soon as we got home that day I called my pediatrician. I said I needed to talk to her about my concerns about Toby. Our appointment was later that week, and I told her about my conversation at the pool. I said, "Since Toby will turn two right when these programs start, I don't want to wait anymore. His speech has been a concern for nine months now. I don't know anything about this Help Me Grow program, but don't you think we should try it?"

She said, "You're right. I wasn't thinking about the timing of his birthday. You should get him in and let's see what they say. I can write you a referral for speech testing, but I think they may do it for free. Why don't you call me if they don't and we'll set you up."

I had no idea I might not need a referral. I never thought they would listen to us without a doctor's request, but it turned out I didn't even need that. I called the main office and they assigned a social worker to our family to coordinate the process. First, they would test Toby. Then, if problems were found, the social worker would help us get enrolled in any therapies Toby might need and check up on him periodically.

We discovered that some babies are enrolled in the program from birth. If you enter the world with certain issues that will obviously affect your development, they sign you up in the hospital and work with you from the beginning of your life. This was the case with my friend's son who was born with cerebral palsy. Others, like Toby, have parents who suspect a problem later and they have to go through the steps of being admitted to the program. After age three, all kids move from the county program to their regular school district which provides special education services from age three through graduation. I now tell parents that a good way to know who to contact for help with their babies is to call the special needs department at their local school district because they will always know the name of the early intervention program in their area.

I was glad that we had a plan of action for Toby, but I was also nervous about what they might find. We had a lot of sadness in our lives, and I didn't need more bad news. What followed were three of the hardest months of my life. They were also the three months that began what I now think of as my "everyday miracles."

CHAPTER 9

Seeking Help

July 2006

The social worker assigned to us from Help Me Grow was named Leigh. I was told it would take about a month for her to come out, but she called me a couple days later and said she'd had a cancellation and could come the next day. She came to our house in mid-July to interview me and observe Toby. She gave us some questionnaires to fill out and then had Toby play a few "games" with her which were really developmental tests, such as stacking blocks and putting beads in a jar.

She told me there were several people we needed to contact to schedule assessments. We needed to get another hearing screen and a speech evaluation for Toby, and we would probably also need to set up a screening with an occupational therapist to assess his fine motor skills and a physical therapist to assess his gross motor skills. Then she had me sign a lot of paperwork and told me she'd get back with me after we had the assessments done.

Over the next couple of days as I started to call all of these places, I realized that getting in to all these specialists was going to take months. The speech therapist had a three month wait, but the office wouldn't even schedule us until the hearing screen had been completed and that office had a four month wait. It went on and on. I started to panic, thinking that by the time we got Toby through all the testing he'd be three and they wouldn't take him anyway!

> **fine motor skills**
>
> the ability to coordinate small muscle movements of the hands and fingers for activities such as writing, cutting, or painting, usually guided by the eyes
>
> **gross motor skills**
>
> the ability to use large muscle groups to coordinate one's body for activities such as walking, jumping, throwing, and maintaining balance

God is so amazing. I called back to schedule the hearing screen and heard, "Well, we can get you an appointment in early November. Oh, wait, well, someone canceled for tomorrow. Do you want that?"

We went in for the hearing screen. The results were questionable because Toby had recently had an ear infection. They told us to come back in a month but gave Toby the okay for the speech evaluation anyway. We called the speech center and were told, "Well, we're scheduling for October, but we just had an appointment open up on Thursday. Would you like that?"

It was miraculous, really. These "coincidences" with scheduling happened over and over again with all of Toby's appointments. A process that should have taken about nine months took only one. Thank you, Lord! On July 31st, Toby had his speech evaluation which showed exactly what we had suspected. Toby was seriously delayed in his speech. His language production at almost two years old was testing in the three to six month range. However, his comprehension was testing at the three-year-old range. Though we still didn't understand why that would happen, this matched our everyday experience. Toby was clearly bright and understood everything we said, but he couldn't respond.

We were still waiting for other test results, but this speech finding was enough to qualify Toby for special needs services through the county. Our social worker, Leigh, came over to discuss our options which would have been numerous if it hadn't been the beginning of August. All of the programs started in September, and most of them were already full.

Toby could attend a school program if we could find him a spot somewhere. We were given a list of school names. The programs all had different specialties and prerequisites, and it was up to us to do the research. If we didn't find him a school spot, his other option was to receive private speech therapy twice a week at a clinic, or once a week in our home. We were really hoping for a school spot. Even though I had never intended to send him to preschool this early, he would essentially be receiving extended group therapy which he needed. Going to the clinic would be one hour of therapy a week, and a school program would be anywhere from five to ten hours a week. Although the school kids would be in a group, the speech therapist told us that was actually better, so we were really hoping we could get him in somewhere.

Leigh told us not to get our hopes up. The school program spots fill up fast, and there were children who had been on wait lists for over a year. Coming into the program late had put us behind all the kids who had been in Help Me Grow since birth, as well as all of the kids who had previously tested.

Most of the school programs were nowhere near our home and many were a forty-five minute drive or more. I really hoped I wouldn't have to drive that far because I didn't know how I would get Toby there and still get the girls to their two schools. Rinnah was starting second grade in the fall and Rachel was in preschool. None of the schedules matched and it looked like it would be impossible to get everyone where they needed to go. I didn't want to shortchange the girls' needs because of Toby's therapies. It was hard to know how to balance it all.

We did find two options that were a good fit. One was a program that sounded so perfect we couldn't believe it existed. It was right at the Columbus Speech and Hearing Center where we'd taken Toby for his hearing screen. They ran a preschool program in one wing of the building that was specifically targeted for kids who were delayed in speech production but not in comprehension. The feedback from parents was amazing. They loved the program and their kids made tremendous progress. It was also only twenty minutes from our home. Unfortunately, they only took two classes of eight kids each year, and both classes were already full. We put Toby on the wait list there, and he was number four on the list. They had only used their wait list once when someone had moved and, in that case, the spot went to the first child.

Our other option was Marburn Academy. Marburn had an excellent reputation and was twenty minutes away, but it also had a wait list. However, we were told that there were more classes in this program and Toby would be more likely to get a spot. The biggest difference between the two programs was that Marburn was generalized for all special needs. The teachers would be trained to work on speech, but they would have children with various issues in the classroom, and the children wouldn't all be working on the same thing. I wasn't sure how I felt about that. I didn't know anything about special education, and the image of my fearful Toby in a classroom with kids in wheelchairs, severe mental delays, or autism didn't seem like the best environment for him to learn how to talk. Of course, the situation isn't like that at all, but I didn't know that. Everyone assured us it was a wonderful program, and we knew there was almost no chance of the other program coming through, so we just tried to be happy that there might be room for him there.

If Toby didn't get into one of those programs, our remaining options were much worse. There were a few programs extremely far away from us that didn't have the same credentialed teachers. There was one that wasn't too bad for distance, but when we looked into it, it was really just child care and we didn't need that – we wanted therapy. We realized that if he didn't get into the Columbus Speech and Hearing Center or Marburn Academy, we'd have to take whatever individual therapy we could get and hope for the best. I wasn't going to put my child in a program that I wasn't very sure of, and even the ones that looked good on paper scared me. This was my baby!

We also looked into our insurance coverage to see if we could get private speech therapy covered. We quickly realized that was a dead end. The only way our insurance would cover speech therapy was if the problem was the direct result of a traumatic injury. We talked to them about Toby's scarring on his ear drums, and how the injury from all his ear infections had contributed to his hearing loss and speech delay, but it was like talking to a brick wall. After pursuing it for a while with our doctor's support, we were finally told that unless there was a car accident or direct head trauma, speech was never covered. End of story.

This was so frustrating. We knew Toby needed speech therapy, and we had been told by medical professionals that his delay was a direct result of the trauma to his ear drums which was a medical condition. Why wouldn't our medical insurance cover his therapy? Nathan and I felt helpless as we realized that even though we'd identified a problem, we didn't have a solution, either through a school program or through private therapy.

We gave it to the Lord. He had made a way for us to get all this testing done quickly, and He knew what Toby needed far better than we did. We knew we could trust God and we would just keep stepping through whatever doors He opened.

A family portrait from that summer

CHAPTER 10

A Sacred Moment

Late July 2006

While all this was happening with Toby, I had also started doing some music ministry. I quickly realized I had gone about it all wrong. Most people sing concerts for a while and then, after building up a fan base, they make an album. We'd made the album never thinking of a fan base, and now we had one. We still couldn't pursue the ministry the way I would have liked. There simply wasn't time, and I didn't want to miss any time we had left with my dad.

I had been invited to a local church for their Sunday morning services to tell my story and sing some of my songs. I talked about Dad and sang, and had so many people approach me afterward. I had no idea at the time how my story would evolve to include Toby as I stood talking to people, protecting Toby at the same time, always holding him in my far arm so they wouldn't try to touch him. I knew that God wanted me to pursue this music ministry more intentionally, but I also knew that this wasn't the time, and God would let us know when and how to do that.

I'd begun to accept the fact that God was not going to heal my dad. I still knew that He could, but at this point, it didn't look like that was going to be His will. I don't know why I knew that, but I accepted it as part of God's grace that He was letting me know so that I could prepare my heart for the loss. It sounds crazy since Dad had been sick for two and a half years at this point, but it still seemed shocking that we were going to lose him.

Nathan was driving me up to sing at another church in Michigan and I lay down to close my eyes for a while. I was thinking about my dad, and I starting writing the song "Godspeed" in my head. The first half of the song was how I was feeling and it was absolutely raw. I remember tears rolling down my cheeks from my closed eyes. I had no idea how I could come to terms with losing Dad, and the song showed it. But then, after writing the first half, I really felt that God said to me, "No, you have this all wrong. You are not saying goodbye because you both love Me and you will see each other again." And so God's answer to me became the second half of the song.

Goodbye.
The world is not a better place.
You've torn an empty, aching space in my heart.
Goodbye.
I know that now your pain is done.
Your life in heaven's just begun,
But I'm still here.

"Sorry for your loss, just give it time.
He's in a better place," yes, but the loss still is mine.
Can you hear those church bells chime?
Marking the march of time,
Oh, the march of time.

Goodbye.
The world is not a better place.
You've torn an empty, aching space in my heart.
Goodbye.
I know that now your pain is done.

Your life in heaven's just begun,
But I'm still here.

He was a godly man who loved the Lord.
But no matter the strength of his love, his God loved him more.
And He held him through the storm,
Across to the other shore, oh, the other shore.

But we don't live like the rest of the world -
We know that this is not the end.
So though I'll grieve your loss to my soul,
I know I'll see you again.

So not goodbye.
For those who love the Lord it's true.
He's prepared a place for you, and for me too.
So not goodbye, no,
'Cause I'll see you on the other side.
And there your arms will open wide
And I'll run in.

I love you. I'll miss you.
But I'll see you again.
This parting is not forever.
Godspeed, my friend.

Dad had asked me to sing at his memorial, but I knew there was no way I could get through it. How could I possibly sing on that day? And yet, I would do anything for my dad. What could I do?

I called Jon, who had made my first album, and asked if he would help me record the new song. I figured then we could play it at the service, and I wouldn't have to sing it live, but Dad would still have my song at his memorial. Hospice had told us that we only had a matter of weeks before Dad passed away. I didn't know what else Jon was working on at the time and I really hoped he'd have at least one day free.

When I called, Jon sounded a bit hesitant, but then said, "I can do it Tuesday night. Can you come then? But we've actually moved the studio. We're downtown now."

I found out afterward that they hadn't moved anything to the new studio when we spoke. Neil and Jon had barely finished packing up their old studio but they never told me. They worked nonstop to get everything moved and set up just to allow me to do that one song. When I got there Tuesday night, they had both stayed up the whole night before getting ready for me. That touched me so much. Jon's mom had died when he was young, and he really understood my need to get this done.

That was one of the hardest things I've ever done. Jon and I worked on it together and laid down individual tracks rather than using a band. No one knew the song anyway because it was all still in my head. Jon played the guitars and bass and I played the piano. Then I had to sing it, and it was so hard to even voice the thoughts I had written. Jon and I didn't talk much. I sat next to him listening at the end of the session while he did a quick mix and master. We were going to clean it up later, but we needed something we could use quickly. When he gave me the disc I noticed he had tears in his eyes. I still can't thank him enough for helping me make that song happen.

I went to my parents' house after the session to play the recording for them. I hadn't even played the song on the piano for them before. I simply couldn't do it. I had learned over the years to divorce my mind from the content of a song if I was singing something really emotional because it was the only way to get my voice to obey me. In this case, though, it was just too much. I simply could not sing this song with my dad in the room with me. So instead I told them I had a recording and played it for them in Dad's room.

We all stared at different corners of the room and didn't make eye contact. I knew if I looked at them I would cry. It was a really long four minutes. At the end of the song none of us spoke for a moment and then my dad said, "It's a really good song, Jenny. Really good. I want that at the service."

That night I stayed and talked to my dad. He was in a serious mood, and he seemed to be having an easier time breathing than usual. We talked about a lot of things, but at the end just before I went home he said, "Jenny, when you become successful with this music, don't forget what's important. Don't ever forget to put God first and to make your family your priority. Don't do things that will compromise your family. Nothing is worth that."

I said, "Dad, I really don't think we have to worry about that. Not because I won't make mistakes, but because I don't think we have to worry about my making some big career out of this."

He looked at me so intently and said, "Yes. You will. This will be successful. And I want you to remember when that happens what you know now. Nothing is more important than God. And nothing on this earth is more important than your family. Don't forget that."

"I won't, Dad. I promise." It stands out in my memory so clearly. It was a sacred moment. And even though I still didn't believe I would "make it big" on any scale, I knew my dad needed to have that said. It felt like a blessing on a new ministry. I knew then that God and I would have to be talking about what He wanted me to do with this music ministry soon.

That memory is so precious to me because those talks didn't happen again. Dad had been having good days and bad days, but now his medication and the oxygen deprivation were making him really groggy and fuzzy. I heard about people having a few more clear, lucid conversations with him after that, but I never caught the moment again. It was the end of July, and it was the last time I really talked with my dad.

CHAPTER 11

Godspeed

August 2006

August arrived. Toby was in testing and we were looking for
therapies for him. My dad was nearing the end of his life.

It was shocking how quickly Dad had deteriorated. He'd always
been one of the strongest people I knew – an athlete with big, hard
hands and muscles. Now his muscles were gone, his chest was sunken
and his stomach stuck out because his abdominal wall couldn't hold it in
anymore. His hands were useless and still, the muscles gone, his fingers
permanently curled. He was in and out of consciousness and every
breath was a struggle. He wrote an entry for his blog one last time at the
beginning of August, but even that was about how he was struggling
with lucidity as he held onto what he knew to be true – Jesus.

It was also shocking to us how quickly Toby was deteriorating. I
didn't know how to describe it except that he seemed to be "shut down."
He had been difficult before, but as long as he was with us and we kept
him from the things that really bothered him, he was mostly happy. Now
his few words were gone and his sounds had disappeared. He was so
afraid of food at this point that we had a hard time getting him to stay in
the room with us while we ate. Our family room and eating area are
together, so we resorted to letting him sit in his red chair watching
television during meals. Afterward, he would eat his three acceptable

Toby in his red chair by the TV

foods and we would give him his supplements. He didn't initiate play at all. He didn't move unless we told him to. He was eerily still and unsmiling a lot of the time.

Still, there were days when things went well for Toby, and that made it possible to keep thinking he might be fine. We took all the kids to a water park one day and Toby went crazy for the kiddie rides. He wanted to ride the little cars that went in a circle over and over. He loved everything about it, and he even swam with us in the little kids' pool. It was wonderful and unpredictable at the same time.

My dad was in a lot of pain. It felt terribly disloyal, but I got to the point that I prayed for it to be over for him. He couldn't breathe and he had no padding anywhere on his body anymore so he ached and had sores. We spent most days at my parents' house and Nathan took turns with my brothers and other men helping Dad during the nights as well. Toby was fine at my parents' house as long as he was with me. It felt like we were all waiting.

In mid-August, Toby had his second hearing screen. It was also inconclusive and they told us to come back in two weeks. They were thinking he would probably need hearing aids, if not on both ears, then at least on the right, but they couldn't confirm. A lot of the trouble with testing was that Toby really couldn't tolerate having headphones on, so it was difficult to tell if his lack of response was because he was fighting that or because he wasn't hearing the sounds.

Our girls were struggling. We had been giving Toby a lot of attention which meant less time for them, and they really didn't understand what was happening to their Papa either. They loved Papa so much, and my parents were a big part of their lives. We were very open about my dad's illness, but they were so young it was hard for them to comprehend. Nathan and I were also struggling with so much sadness, and that was disorienting for Rinnah and Rachel. Parents are supposed to be able to fix things, and we couldn't fix any of this.

It was Monday, August 28th. We were at my parents' house and my dad wasn't conscious. He hadn't been conscious when we'd been there for a few weeks at that point, but this was terrible. He was moaning even in his sleep and he was in such pain. I wouldn't let the girls go in to see him, and I called his doctor and asked him to please come and do something. No one should be moaning from pain while unconscious and on that much morphine.

My dad's doctor was amazing. He was one of the busiest doctors in the city, but he still came over personally that afternoon while we were there and worked with the hospice nurse on Dad's dosing. Rinnah was so sad that day and wanted to go in and see her Papa. I told her she might be able to if they could make him more comfortable. Her words brought me up short. "Okay, Mommy, but when is Papa going to wake up and play dominoes with me again? I've been waiting and waiting."

I realized that she didn't know. I had no idea. We had told our girls that Papa was dying and he had been sick for a long time, but Rinnah didn't realize that Papa was really going to die, and it was going to be soon.

I said, "Honey, Papa isn't going to wake up again. He is dying, and his body just can't wake up right now."

She said, "What do you mean he's not going to wake up? Not today? Or not ever?"

"I'm so sorry, sweetie, but he's not going to wake up again."

"He's dying now? Right now? It's happening now?" She was starting to get hysterical.

"Sweetheart, we don't know exactly when, but soon. And he can't wake up again."

Rinnah broke away from me and ran into my dad's room, crying and pleading with him to wake up. My dad's doctor caught her and hugged her and then handed her to me. I carried her out and she cried for an hour while I held her in the other room. After a while, the hospice nurse came out and told me they had grief counseling services for children. She asked if she could have someone come to the house and talk to my girls.

I said, "Sure, maybe we can do that sometime next week."

She replied, "I can have someone here tomorrow. How about tomorrow?" I didn't realize the significance of what she was saying.

Rinnah had to be somewhere after school the next day so I said no. She said, "All right. I'll have someone here Wednesday after school. Is that okay?"

I told her they didn't have to come so soon, and they shouldn't go to so much trouble for us but she insisted. I said, "Okay, thank you, that's fine, Wednesday. I'll bring the girls."

Wednesday afternoon, August 30th, the girls met with the grief counselor in my parents' living room while I sat with my dad. He looked awful. It was almost hard to recognize him. The counselor came in and asked to speak with me. She said that Rinnah had told her that the one thing she wanted to do was to get in bed with Papa and hug him, but Rinnah was afraid she'd hurt him, and she'd been afraid to ask. Rachel said she wanted to do that too. We talked to the hospice nurse, and she said he wasn't going to feel any pain at that point, he was so deeply unconscious.

So I went out and talked to Rinnah and asked if that was what she wanted to do and she said it was. I said it was fine and Papa would love to have a hug. So she lay down carefully on the side of his hospital bed and wrapped her arms around him. I thought I should get the camera and take a picture for her to have. Then I thought, no, I'll bring the camera tomorrow or next week, I won't bother now. Then I felt, "No, go get it." It was like a small voice. "You should do that, you'll want it."

I ran home. We only live a few blocks from my parents so I was gone less than three minutes. Rinnah hadn't moved so I took a picture of her and Papa. She laid there with him for about twenty minutes, hugging him and whispering in his ear. Then Rachel asked for a turn and did the same thing and I took a picture for her too.

I took the girls into the kitchen while my mom sat with my dad and asked them what they had said to Papa. They both said they had told him how much they loved him and that they would miss him and they hoped he would feel better. We'd been in the kitchen only about fifteen minutes when my mom cried out for us. My dad's brother was there and he ran back. I told Rinnah and Rachel to stay in the kitchen, and I ran back too. My dad was gone. I truly believe he had been waiting for the girls because he somehow knew they needed to say goodbye.

Within minutes the whole family was there. Dad had gone peacefully. When he was a child, he'd had terrible asthma, and the only thing he really feared was not being able to breathe. We were so grateful that he had not struggled. And we knew that he was free. He was free from this disease, he was free from this body, and he was with Jesus who loved him and walked him through it all.

It was the only time I got angry. Right there, standing in the sun room with the light streaming in, looking at my dad's body, I felt a sudden wave of rage sweep over me. I was furious with ALS! How dare it! How dare it take my dad! How could it overcome this vibrant, vital, brilliant, courageous man! It was unthinkable, and I just wanted to throw all the bottles of pills and the wires and the machines and scream and stamp and hurt something! How could you? How could you!

And slowly, like a quiet whisper in my mind, God reminded me that He was with me. That He loved Dad more than I did, and that He had a purpose. That He would not leave us alone. That He would use this time if I would just let Him. That He would be with my mom, my kids, my brothers, and my nieces and nephews. God was our Rock and our Fortress, an ever-present help in trouble.

Revelation 21:3-4 says, speaking about the time when Christ will return, "Now the dwelling of God is with men, and he will live with them. They will be his people, and God himself will be with them and be their God. He will wipe every tear from their eyes. There will be no more death or mourning or crying or pain, for the old order of things has passed away." How I longed for this day – and Dad was already there! He would have no more mourning or crying or pain. No more death. Alleluia.

That time with Dad and Toby felt as though I was falling down a pit. I was off center all the time, and I didn't know as I was falling how deep this pit was or how badly it would hurt when I hit the bottom. Would I be broken? Could I recover? Would it kill me? I didn't know. But when I did hit the bottom, the only way to describe it is to say that God caught me. He was there. It was still a pit, but I wasn't alone there. One of the most precious names for God to me is "Emmanuel" which means "God with us." God is with us. And God was with me. Praise God.

We had an amazing memorial service. Over a thousand people came to the calling hours. A thousand more came to the service. Dad had touched a lot of lives. Later, we had a small family service to bury his ashes. He was buried on his birthday, September 5th, 2006. He would have been fifty-nine years old.

CHAPTER 12

A Place for Toby

September 2006

A fter Dad's death, I found myself in a fog. It's hard to focus on that time because it's hazy in my memory. We'd known for a long time that Dad was going to die, and I thought that I had somehow dealt with some of the grief beforehand. When he passed away, I realized that hadn't happened. It was just a different grief. Even though we'd been told there was no hope, that there were no survivors, I was still surprised. I didn't realize until he was gone that I had held onto the hope that he wouldn't really die.

One of the ways I seem to deal with grief is to not think about it. I stuff everything down and move on. Then, occasionally, when I think I can handle it, I'll take out a little piece of it and try to process it. I don't think this is the best method. It explains why now, almost five years later, I will almost instantly cry if I am unexpectedly reminded of my dad. But still, it's what I do.

I managed to suppress a lot of my pain from Dad's death and Toby's struggles and move on. Maybe I didn't do it as well as I thought I had. My husband told me that I was fairly vacant there for a while, and would spend time looking for things that were right in front of me. Sometimes I would not quite understand what people were saying to me, and I went through a period of real depression. I was in survival mode at that point.

In mid-September we had planned a short family trip organized around a couple of singing events I had in Florida. It seems crazy to me now that we went, but we didn't want to disappoint the kids or the churches who had scheduled me to sing. It also appeared to be a great opportunity to run away from some of the pain and struggle at home. Of course, that never works, but it seemed like a good plan at the time.

During that trip, we made the fateful visit to the beach where Toby panicked and cried at just the sight of sand and water, and I realized he really wasn't okay. Things weren't getting better, they were getting worse. He was shutting down. It wasn't just speech delay. There were so many symptoms and strange behaviors. How did they fit together? Were they even related? Would he ever speak? Would he ever be able to function normally? Was this decline we were seeing able to be halted or would he continue to worsen? Was he autistic? I still didn't think it was autism, but I knew of nothing else with so many of the markers I was seeing.

At this dark time in my life, I really didn't know what to do. I had never been so emotionally and physically exhausted. There were so many needs with my mom and my kids grieving. I was grieving. After facing everything with my dad, how could I face a new fight with Toby when I didn't even know what we were fighting against?

I'd like to say that I turned it all over to God and had a great spiritual epiphany. The truth was that I was so spent, I couldn't even think of that possibility. I was simply trying to survive the day. And yet, God ordered our steps. He knew we were at the end of our rope, and so doors opened, things happened, and we just blindly kept walking, placing one foot in front of the other.

We still hadn't heard from the programs at Marburn Academy or at Columbus Speech and Hearing Center (CSHC) and we knew that both of the programs were starting up at that time. I had checked in again before we left for Florida and our social worker, Leigh, told me she hadn't called CSHC because the chances of Toby getting in there were so small, but that Marburn said he had moved up the list enough that they might be able to take him mid-year. We weren't very happy with that, especially since he would start as the new kid in an established class, but we didn't have other options. In the meantime, we were going to start the private speech therapy offered by the county as soon as we got back, and pray for a school spot to open up sooner rather than later.

Imagine my surprise when we returned home from our trip and I had a message from CSHC. Somehow they had four spots fall through in their afternoon program. Two children had moved, and another child's parents had decided they wanted him exclusively in private therapy. The fourth child had started the program, but since it was exactly when almost every two-year-old is napping, his parents felt it was just too disruptive to his schedule and pulled him out. That left a space for Toby in a program that had only ever used one spot on its wait list in the program's history.

How in the world had we received this impossible placement? I knew it was God. He had directed all those random cancellations that had let us finish the testing so quickly. He had somehow moved Toby up the wait list. God knew what Toby needed and He was putting Toby where he needed to be.

I was terrified that the spot might now be taken. I didn't know when they had left the message. I called immediately and was connected to Stacey Gall, the CSHC preschool director and one of the speech therapists there. She would also be one of the teachers in Toby's class. They had only called the day before, and she asked if Toby could please come in the following Monday for intake testing and then start the program on Wednesday. What an answer to prayer!

When we arrived at CSHC on Monday, they already had Toby's previous speech assessment and hearing screens. A subsequent screen showed his hearing was in the normal range, so he would not need more surgery or hearing aids. Praise the Lord! Later that month, Toby would fail another hearing test at his annual check-up, but we were told it was because he was borderline at that point. Some days he would fail and some days he would pass, but on average he appeared to be hearing well enough to learn to speak.

They gave him another speech assessment and determined that at this point he could make twenty sounds. He was also "jargoning" which meant that he used repetitive phrases with the same intonation as speech and with the intent to communicate, but without actually saying words. He would say, "Duh-kah-duh-kah-duh-kah? Duh-kah-duh-kah. Duh-KAH!" and he was really trying to ask a question or share something. He was imitating speech patterns as well as he could, but his mouth wasn't cooperating.

Toby thought the intake testing was a lot of fun. They played many of the same games with him that Leigh had at our initial meeting. They took him to the play kitchen area and the block area and colored with him and looked at books, all the while letting me stay nearby. He looked for me every few moments, but, since I was there and didn't seem to be going anywhere, he just enjoyed himself. They offered him a snack which he violently refused, but they didn't push it so he went happily back to playing. Then we went to what would become one of his favorite places in the world – the OT gym.

I had never heard of occupational therapy (OT) and really didn't know much about it until Toby had been at the preschool for a while. Essentially, OT helps people develop the skills needed to accomplish their everyday tasks. For preschoolers, this means anything supporting the ability to effectively play and learn, such as fine motor skills, motor planning, eating, or sensory processing.

> **motor planning**
>
> the ability to conceptualize, plan, and execute complex tasks involving fine and/or gross motor skills
>
> For example, simply putting on a shirt involves thinking of all the motions involving your hands, arms, head, and torso, and then directing your body to go through those motions.

The OT gym was just like an indoor playground. This gym had a ball pit, several varieties of swings, a jumping pole, a climbing wall, all shapes and sizes of mats and tubes and blocks that could be made into obstacle courses as well as games and riding toys. It wasn't a large space, but it was amazing what they had done with it. Toby loved this place! There were no messy things. Everything had a smooth texture, and it was padded so he could fall without getting hurt. He could play with everything! He was in heaven. He played with the occupational therapist for quite a while, again checking for me often, and then we were done for the day.

The ball pit in the OT gym

Now that I had seen the program in person, I was so excited. I hadn't known what to expect, but this was such a bright, happy, and above all, completely *normal* feeling preschool. There was nothing sad or institutional about it. The teachers seemed great and the kids were having fun. Toby himself seemed so happy. He had interacted with everyone and had even smiled and played. I hadn't seen that in a while. I felt a breath of hope. Maybe something would actually work for Toby here.

While we were there, I asked why there was an occupational therapist on staff at a school which specialized in speech delay. They said that a major factor in speech delay in children is often sensory processing disorder which is addressed with occupational therapy. I didn't really think about it much more. I hadn't heard of the disorder, and since we had been admitted to the program so late, we focused on getting Toby settled. I thought I'd ask more about it later. For now, though, it looked like this school was the best placement we could have hoped for. And since Toby loved the OT gym so much, he couldn't wait to come back!

CHAPTER 13

A New World

Late September 2006

T he other children in Toby's class at CSHC had started the program
gradually. They stayed only an hour on their first day, slowly
building up to the full two and a half hours over two weeks. Toby had
missed that transitional time, but the teachers told us to come back on
Wednesday to stay for an hour of the program, and we would do an
abbreviated version of that transition.

Every kid had his or her own picture symbol and Toby chose a
teddy bear. The bear was put on his mailbox, on his cup, on his
attendance box, and anything else that belonged to him. They also sent a
couple bear stickers home with us so we could label his room or other
belongings. It was one of the first ways they helped the kids to
communicate without words. They could use the symbols for each other.
The therapists explained that the more the children could communicate
by any method, the more confidence they gained to try to speak, and the
less frustration they experienced in general, which also helped the
learning process. It was amazing that all the children learned the symbols
within two days. It was very sweet how they would find another child's
cup and return it to them, or sort the mail by their pictures.

One thing I loved about the program was that the classroom and
the OT gym both had small, attached observation rooms with one-way

glass and a speaker system. The parents could sit in there and watch and hear the class without their kids seeing them and becoming upset by the separation. Many of the parents watched most days. It was so helpful because we could see how our kids were doing, what methods were successful, and what to do at home. It was also great because we all came to know each other and could share stories of what was working for us at home. We didn't feel so alone. Suddenly, we realized there were other parents and children struggling with the same issues, and it really helped.

The program ran four days a week from 1:00 PM to 3:30 PM. There were eight kids in the class, and it was taught every day by a speech therapist and a child development specialist. In addition, we often had at least one volunteer, as well as a student teacher studying speech or occupational therapy. Our occupational therapist taught one day each week and set up therapies for the other days. All in all, we usually had four or five adults in the room with our eight kids. It was amazing.

I was humbled and touched by the depth of caring these professionals had for our children. These people were highly trained, and their expertise was apparent. And yet, they absolutely loved our kids. This was not clinical for them. The teachers would get down on the floor and blow bubbles and jabber with the kids. They would learn what each child liked and didn't like. They would learn all of their siblings' and pets' names and what they did when they weren't in school. Therapeutically, it was so they could talk to them about all those things, but they also really cared. They were made for preschoolers!

Often, if I would report a small victory to Toby's speech therapist, Stacey, during that year, she would tear up because she was so happy for us and so proud of Toby. Nothing was too small to share with her; she was interested in everything. It was the same with Jessie, his development specialist, and Angie, his occupational therapist. He loved them all and he knew they loved him back.

For all of that, it was still a rough transition to school. Toby was in the afternoon class, and he had been on a strict schedule that had him

Toby with his speech therapist, Stacey

sleeping at exactly the same time as the program. He really needed a nap. After all, he was only two! We thought it was worth the sacrifice, though, and our days took on a strange pattern. Toby and Rachel were both in a kid's Bible class two mornings a week that year while I had Bible study. On those days we would leave Bible study at 11:15 AM and eat lunch in the car. Then I would drive around at random until Toby fell asleep. Rachel and I learned all the neighborhoods around her preschool! Then at 12:30 PM, I would take Rachel to preschool and she would crawl silently out of the car at the drop-off line so she wouldn't wake Toby up. Then I would drive up to CSHC and let him sleep a few more minutes in the parking garage until his class was starting. He usually got at least an hour nap this way which made it possible for him to make it through school, although for the first several weeks the teachers kept finding children, Toby included, asleep in the book corner.

After an hour and fifteen minutes, I'd leave to pick up Rinnah at the elementary school at 2:30 PM, then Rachel at the preschool at 3:00 PM, and then back to CSHC to pick up Toby at 3:30 PM. I was grateful that it was possible to get them all where they needed to be, but the schedule was tough. It meant that I couldn't do anything else between 11:45 AM and 4:00 PM every day. I was also sorry to miss half of Toby's therapy every day since I wanted to learn everything I could. The second half of class was always snack time, and food was an area we were really struggling with at home. As the year went on, some of the other parents who were able to stay for the whole class started watching Toby at snack time for me and reporting what had happened when I got back to pick him up. I really appreciated that. Toby would then take a short nap in the car on the way home, and we'd do it again the next day. I was always so touched by Rinnah and Rachel's patience with it all. They spent a lot of time in the car that year being quiet for Toby, and were so good about it and happy to help him.

A typical day at the preschool would start with goodbyes at the door. Toby had a very hard time separating from me for several weeks, and the staff let me stay with him in the class for a few days until I could gradually begin to leave. It was important therapeutically for Toby to be there without me, but it was also important to the teachers that the separation was not traumatic. It always broke my heart when Toby was scared or crying, and they made the transition as gentle as possible for him. Toby was allowed to come and knock on the one-way window whenever he was worried I wasn't waiting for him and I would knock back. Many of the kids did this, and of course, someone in the room would knock if a parent had stepped out. The kids couldn't see in, they just knew the parents waited in there, and it reassured them.

After goodbyes, the children would have free play for a while. Then there was a circle time. The kids' pictures were on magnets, and the teachers would always call up each child one by one to stick their picture on the board if they were there, and together the group would say each child's name. Many of those kids' names were the first words Toby tried to say. There was never a wasted moment in that classroom and every single thing was therapeutic, but I loved that the kids had no idea. They just thought their preschool was a lot of fun.

During circle time they had a story and sometimes a game and then the children would have more free play including things like crafts and books and imaginative play. Half the kids would go to the OT gym and then they would switch. If it was nice weather they would all go to the outdoor playground. Then they would have snack time, a final circle and their goodbye song, and all the kids would go home.

I learned so much about speech just from watching that class. Stacey would brush their teeth, which I thought was strange since the kids were only there a couple of hours total. Why would they need to brush their teeth? Well, they didn't. Stacey explained that the toothbrush was used to help them learn the different parts of their mouths and how to use them. She would even have them practicing different mouth shapes or sounds while they were spitting. Everything was a game, and everything had a purpose.

I knew that snack time was going to be a real challenge for Toby. I had told them that Toby was an extremely picky eater and very resistant to new foods of any kind. I didn't understand why they even needed snack. Couldn't Toby just skip that part? Snack time would only upset him and make it harder for him to learn.

Stacey talked through the reasoning behind snack time with the parents, and it quickly became apparent in many ways why it was an integral part of the class. She told us she was not going to teach them manners, she was going to help them speak. She told the kids that these were "preschool manners" but they had to use the manners mom and dad taught them everywhere else. Then she would have them balancing Cheerios on the tips of their tongues or showing food to each other. The kids thought it was hilarious to play with their food. Everything exercised a different muscle group or part of their mouths, making it easier for them to coordinate their mouths to talk. She explained that most speech delayed kids thought their mouth was just a black hole and didn't even know how to begin to speak until they knew all the parts they were working with: the tongue, the lips, the cheeks, the teeth. They had to figure this mouth thing out first before they could begin talking!

Stacey also told us that snack was therapeutic for the kids who were struggling with sensory disorders. There was that phrase again. I immediately tuned into that because I didn't know any child who had a harder time with food than Toby. She didn't elaborate at the time, but I made a mental note to ask her what that meant after class sometime soon.

Toby was not enamored with snack time. They did it family style, sitting in chairs around a table, and everyone had the same food. The first few times, they had "safe" snacks – Cheerios and graham crackers. These foods are not intimidating for most kids. However, after the first week or so, they added some chocolate pudding. Most kids would love that, but not Toby. They put a dime-sized dollop on his plate and he gasped and stared at them like they had betrayed him. He scrambled out of his chair so fast he knocked it over backwards and ran for the door. He was literally hanging from the handle trying to escape.

His teacher, Jessie, came over and told him it was okay. He didn't have to eat it. They were just going to let it sit there and he didn't have to touch it. After several minutes he finally went back to the table with her, but he wouldn't sit down again or get close to it. He just stood behind Jessie's chair looking ready to fly at any moment. Stacey came out afterward and said that perhaps Toby's food aversion was more severe than they had realized. That was an understatement! It was at this point that the occupational therapist, Angie, asked if we could schedule a meeting.

CHAPTER 14

Another Diagnosis

October 2006

A ngie sat down with me and asked if I'd ever heard of sensory integration dysfunction or sensory processing disorder (SPD). It was a relatively new diagnosis, and there was still some disagreement over what it should be called, but they were the same thing. I told her I'd never heard of it.

She began to describe it to me. SPD is a neurological condition where the brain has difficulty processing sensory input. There were seven sensory systems that could be affected. The first five were the ones everyone thinks of as their senses: taste, touch, hearing, sight, and smell. The last two were areas I hadn't heard of or thought about as sensory systems. The proprioceptive system delivers input to the brain from the muscles and joints. The vestibular system gives input to the brain from the inner ear and deals with balance and knowing where the body is in space. All of these sensory systems work together to deliver information to the brain and help it to perceive the world and where one is in it.

When a person has SPD, their brain is not processing sensory input correctly. Sometimes it is misread or not read at all. It could affect just one of those systems or all of them, although more commonly it would affect at least a few and there is some overlap between certain systems such as taste and smell. The brain could also react either too much to the

seven sensory systems

sight, sound, taste, smell, touch or tactile, proprioception (awareness of body position and input to muscles and joints), and vestibular (awareness of head position and movement which is critical for balance)

* See Appendix A for more details on the sensory systems.

input, or not enough. With all these variables, children and adults with the disorder can have very different symptoms.

Most people have some sensory sensitivities. Maybe they don't like a certain texture on their hands, or a specific food in their mouths. Perhaps they can't stand the sound of fingernails on a chalkboard, or they don't like having their hair brushed. None of those sensitivities are by themselves anything to worry about. But when the sensory issues start to interfere with development or learning, it crosses the line into a disorder.

People can have difficulty interpreting sensory input on either end of a spectrum; they either overreact to input or underreact to it. Angie started to describe some of the symptoms of SPD; speech delay, extremely picky or extremely messy eating, sensitivity to clothing and textures, poor balance, sensitivity to noise or visual stimulation, over-reaction or no reaction to touch, unusually high tolerance for or sensitivity to pain, avoiding motion or seeking constant motion including spinning and swinging. There were many more, and as she was talking, my heart started pounding. I was thinking, "Check, check, check. This is it! That's my Toby! This is the problem, and now we have a name!"

My greatest fear was that Toby had severe autism and would continue to deteriorate until he couldn't connect with us anymore. I voiced the question that had been in my heart since our first awareness that something was wrong. "Is this disorder related to autism?" I asked. I desperately needed to know.

"Sensory integration is the neurological process that organizes sensations from one's body and from the environment, and makes it possible to use the body to make adaptive responses within the environment. To do this, the brain must register, select, interpret, compare, and associate sensory information in a flexible, constantly-changing pattern." A. Jean Ayres, 1989

Angie told me that the jury was still out on that. The experts are still debating this topic at the time of the writing of this book. Autism is a spectrum disorder, meaning that there are many levels of severity and forms that it can take. Classifying SPD as an autism spectrum disorder had been discussed, but had not happened. At the time, the understanding was that autistic children almost always have issues with sensory processing, but it was possible to have SPD and not be autistic. Because of this connection, many of the symptoms of SPD also are indicators of autism. However, SPD does not also include the social and emotional markers which differentiate autism.

Angie said, "It's too early to determine or worry about autism in Toby. I don't see it, but he is very young. I think we should work on his sensory processing and see where it goes. This should really help his speech as well." Apparently sensory processing issues kept children with the disorder so focused on just getting through their days that they didn't have enough capacity left over to learn the skills needed to meet their developmental milestones. Because of this, SPD can be a major contributor to many delays, including speech delay.

We left the meeting that day with new answers, but new questions as well. It was hard not to have a definite answer about the possibility of autism. It had been in the back of my mind for a long time. And now that we had a diagnosis, what did we do with it? What did I know about SPD anyway? Could it be cured? Would Toby continue to get worse? What was the treatment like?

My mind was just spinning. I had so many questions, and I'd already had so many for such a long time! I turned to God. He is peace when there is none. It says in John 16:33, "In this world, you will have trouble. But take heart! I have overcome the world." My fears and sadness about Toby's situation were problems I had to give to God every single day. God had taken care of us when my dad was dying and when we lost the baby. I knew He loved Toby and that we could trust Him with Toby's future. Life is not always the way we want it to be, but I truly knew that God works things together for good (Romans 8:28). There has never been anything harder than trusting Him with my child, but there is also no one more trustworthy. As I confirmed these truths about God and His character, He gave me peace in what felt like this storm of emotion I had been enduring. All of His promises are true.

As soon as we had the diagnosis, we started learning everything we could about the disorder. Since SPD was a fairly new diagnosis, there wasn't a lot of literature on it. One of the first books on the subject was *The Out-of-Sync Child* by Carol Stock Kranowitz. I read it immediately, and so many things became clearer. Children with SPD are not able to interpret and integrate sensory input correctly. The disorder can go in both directions; sometimes the children overreact to input, and sometimes they underreact. In many cases, the children have one response in one area and a different response in another, so the child may be a very picky eater, but have an uncommon tolerance for pain at the same time.

In Toby's case, he was extremely hypersensitive to touch and his vestibular system was not functioning well, perhaps in part due to the severity of his ear infections affecting his inner ear. All of a sudden it became clear that these seemingly unrelated issues – Toby's speech, eating, clothing preferences, balance troubles – were just parts of this one larger problem. It was as if the symptoms were the tip of the iceberg we could see poking out of the water, but the iceberg itself was SPD.

When we looked at his behavior, we realized it was all a response to this problem. Toby couldn't talk, so he couldn't tell us. And even if he had been able to communicate the problem, it was all he had ever known. He wouldn't have had an awareness that it wasn't the way it should be. When he cried in fear about food, it was because it hurt his mouth, it was intolerable for him. When he refused to put on a certain shirt or change shoes, it was because he couldn't stand that touch. The reason he wouldn't get up and play was because he was afraid he would fall.

Carol Stock Kranowitz has an interesting quote on her website. "Many parents, educators, doctors, and mental health professionals have difficulty recognizing SPD. When they don't recognize the problem, they may mistake a child's behavior, low self-esteem, or reluctance to participate in ordinary childhood experiences for hyperactivity, learning disabilities, or emotional problems. Unless they are educated about SPD, few people understand that bewildering behavior may stem from a poorly functioning nervous system."

I knew it! I knew Toby wasn't being "bad." He simply couldn't do the things we were trying to get him to do. I knew there were foods he wanted to try, but he just couldn't. I knew he was a happy, easy-going boy inside, but he was unable to function that way.

We saw so many things in a different light. For instance, now I understood his attachment to the red chair and the television. Because his hearing wasn't good, he didn't always know when people were coming up behind him. The occupational therapist described light touch for Toby like sparks down his skin. When he sat in the red chair, it went all the way around him. It protected him. People couldn't surprise him with a touch before he saw them. Visual stimulation was safe for him, so he loved the television. Television was fun without movement, and he was always hurting himself when he moved because his vestibular system wasn't working. Put all those things together, and his favorite place became his safe red chair right in front of the visually stimulating television.

I was amazed at how much it helped just to know what the problem was. It changed our parenting completely. Now we understood Toby's behavior rather than just getting frustrated with him. And because he knew we understood him, he felt safer and started to relax. We could see the relief on his face. It was as if he was saying, "Finally, someone gets it!" He had become increasingly frustrated and angry that summer and fall, and our new understanding of him let the pressure off immediately. His personality started coming through and the atmosphere in our house improved tremendously.

One example of this was my reaction to Toby crying when we parked the car. I had never understood this behavior. It didn't happen every time and it seemed random. He never cried when we parked in the garage at home. I just thought it was because he liked to be home. But he often cried when we parked other places, and he would point out the window at the trees to show me what was distressing him, but I didn't get it. Why would anyone be afraid of a tree? After realizing what was happening with his sensory system, it hit me. The wind hurt. The wind was hurting him, and when the trees branches were waving, he knew it was windy. When we parked the car, he knew we were getting out and it was going to hurt. Wind was light touch, like sparks going up his skin. No wonder he cried!

In the past I would just get frustrated. I cringe to think of it now. "Buddy, come on! We have to get out. Knock it off!" Now that we knew, we could change our approach. "Hey buddy, yeah, it's a little windy today isn't it? Let's put your jacket on. We'll zip it up and I'll hold you so you can put your face on my shoulder and we'll run in. It'll be fine. We'll do it quick and the jacket will help your arms." He knew that I understood what he was feeling. He was so much calmer because he knew we had a plan, and that the plan would actually help.

When I thought back to that day on the beach in Florida, it was unsettling. We couldn't have combined more terrifying things for Toby in one place if we'd tried. Drops of water felt like they were burning him, and there was an ocean. Crumbs and messiness were absolutely intolerable to him and there was a whole beach worth of sand. Even a breeze hurt his skin and the palm branches were whipping in the wind. No wonder Toby lost it! And he couldn't tell us. He was so frustrated and hopeless, he was shutting down. Forget speaking, that was the least of his worries.

I asked the occupational therapist why Nathan and I could always touch Toby. Why didn't that hurt him, but he would never let anyone else near him? She said, "Remember, parents are really in tune with their kids. When you nursed Toby and held him all the time as a baby, you responded to every little thing that made him happy or sad, and you adjusted how you held him in response. Think about it. Do you ever touch Toby lightly? Do you ever ruffle his hair? Are you ever unpredictable with him? No. He knows how you're going to touch him and you are safe."

She was right. I always held Toby firmly, although I'd never noticed it before or done it consciously. Firm touch was fine with him. It was the light and unpredictable sensations that would make him panic. We could hold him and let him "fall" over backwards and swing him upside down and he thought it was great. But if the lady in the nursery at church brushed his arm, or a kid got too close and he didn't know exactly what they were going to do next, he would cry. When he was hurt, which happened often because he was so hypersensitive to pain, he wanted a good hard hug, not gentle patting.

Now that we knew about Toby's SPD, I was worried that we were only addressing his speech. The program at CSHC had been very clear that it was specifically designed for speech delayed kids, not kids dealing with other issues. Would he be kicked out of his new school? I asked Stacey about it, and she said, "No, he's right where he needs to be. This program is perfect for him because we will address both the speech and the sensory processing. But you may want to look into private therapy as well."

As we learned more about SPD, we became aware of the importance of early intervention, preferably between the ages of zero and three. During this time, children's brains are developing rapidly and are still quite malleable. Therapy done during this period can literally re-wire the brain, in essence correcting the problem. After that window closes, gains can still be made, but they happen less quickly and are harder fought. Beyond a certain age, the therapy may focus more on coping with the problem rather than correcting it.

> ## a note for parents
>
> Please know that there is help for older children as well as those identified at a younger age. Early intervention is ideal but therapy is still worth pursuing even if your child's needs were not recognized until an older age. The advice to take a wait-and-see approach is widespread. Please understand it is not too late, there is still hope, and gains can be made!
>
> * Please see Appendix C for further discussion of this topic.

Could it actually be a blessing that Toby's case was so severe? I knew that we would never have gotten it diagnosed so young if that hadn't been the case. I would have kept wondering and waiting, and we would have missed this early intervention window. The majority of SPD cases are much milder, and usually aren't diagnosed until the children are six or seven years old and start to experience problems in school.

We were determined to get as much therapy as we possibly could for Toby while he was in this early intervention window. He started the program at CSHC at twenty-four months old. That gave us a year, or at most a year and a half before the window closed. We wanted to pack as much help into that time frame as possible. Nathan and I watched as many of Toby's classes as we could and asked questions of all the therapists. Why did they do that? How did it help? How could we do this at home?

We tried to reproduce everything that was helping Toby at school in our home as well. It is interesting that, without exception, therapists we have worked with over the years have noted that one of the most significant factors to a positive prognosis for a child is having involved and supportive parents. Parents are their child's most effective advocates, and must take this seriously if they want to see the best possible outcome for their child.

There are no medications or drugs used to treat sensory processing disorder. It is treated with occupational therapy which, in the case of young children, is often largely play-based. The idea is to expose a child to the sensory input his body needs to help his brain make the correct connections and re-map areas of difficulty.

Not everything worked for us. One of the more common therapies for children with tactile issues is brushing. The parent or therapist takes a very soft bristled brush and rubs it in a prescribed way for a certain amount of time over the child's arms and legs, and sometimes torso and back. For many children, this works really well to reorganize their sensory system and make them ready for learning. For Toby, brushing was just a disaster. He was so hypersensitive to touch that he couldn't handle that level of input. It was completely overwhelming. He tolerated it for the first two days, but his reactions to each session became significantly worse. He was getting teary and simply couldn't stand it. We stopped within two weeks.

This was an important lesson. Not every therapy works for every child. We needed to use wisdom working with Toby and go with the things that specifically benefited him. His nervous system couldn't handle that therapy, but there were many other techniques we could try. Over time we were able to find so many things that did help him. The easiest and most effective was simply giving him a huge hug. It was full body tactile input and it always helped his anxiety. Plus, it was socially acceptable in any situation, and far less noticeable than rubbing his arms, legs, and torso with a brush if he needed help in a public situation!

After our stalemate with the insurance company in regard to private speech therapy, I didn't think it was even worth inquiring about private occupational therapy. After a month or so, though, I changed my mind and thought there couldn't be any harm in asking. We were amazed when we found we could schedule forty visits a year with only a co-pay. I couldn't believe it! Apparently this is a fairly common feature of health insurance plans. Alleluia! Once we accounted for school breaks and the occasional illness, forty visits would cover weekly sessions for most of the year! There was a wait list for private occupational therapy at CSHC, but we got on it right away and were told the wait wouldn't be too long.

After Toby's initial diagnosis at the school, his progress was nothing short of miraculous. It was like my little boy had been imprisoned in his own body, and they were able to set him free. I will never forget one morning in October after we started the program. Toby was sitting in his red chair watching television as I did the dishes in the kitchen. I heard the television switch off suddenly, and I looked up to see Toby standing next to it. He had gotten out of his chair and turned off the TV. I couldn't remember that ever happening before. Then he went over to the toy corner and got some wooden blocks out. He sat down and started slowly tapping them together and then stacking them. Toby was playing with blocks. He was playing! I couldn't believe my eyes.

The changes weren't instantaneous, but it sometimes felt as though they were. In fact, his speech improved so quickly that it left us unprepared in some ways for the fight we would still have with Toby's sensory issues. We had begun to think everything would be all better with the snap of our fingers.

Toby started the program with just a few sounds and no words in late September. Four weeks later I was reading him his bedtime story. We were sitting in the rocking chair and I held him on my lap. I finished reading, prayed with him, hugged him and told him I loved him just as I did every night. He turned around in my lap and patted my cheek and said, so slurred, but clear as day to me, "I love you, Mom." I was stunned. I couldn't imagine I'd heard him correctly, but there it was.

"Oh, buddy, I love you too!" I cried and held him so tightly. I really hadn't known if I would ever hear those words. How could I ever thank Toby's therapists? How could I ever thank God enough?

Two weeks later, Toby's class went on a field trip to a pumpkin farm. It was pretty cold, and he wasn't sure if he was going to like the hayride (hay is poky!) or the animals (they are unpredictable!) or the snacks (don't get that cider near me!!) but he still had a great time. At the end of the visit, we went to pick out our pumpkins from the pumpkin patch, and Toby yelled with such excitement, "Is a 'unkin! Is a 'unkin!" He was having what Stacey called a "word explosion" and he would pick up nearly a hundred words before Christmas.

**Jennifer and Toby on the hayride at
the pumpkin farm**

CHAPTER 15

A New Direction
Fall 2006

That entire fall we had been receiving emails from unexpected places about my music. I was happy that people liked it, but we weren't sure where they were coming across the songs. I had my own website and my music was on a few others as well. We assumed they were finding my songs from one of those locations and didn't give it much more thought.

Later we received our first royalty check from ASCAP. ASCAP is the American Society of Composers, Authors and Publishers and is a performance rights organization that I had joined when I made my first album. They distribute royalties to artists if someone uses their music. It was a really small check, but the interesting thing was that I was being paid a royalty because one of my songs was used for a Romanian television show. What in the world? How had they even heard my song in the first place?

I still don't know, actually. But we began to get mail from all over the world: South Africa, Thailand, Australia, England, all over the U.S. and Canada. It wasn't a lot, but it was steady, and I couldn't figure out how all these people were finding my music.

We finally thought to contact the radio service we had registered with months ago. With everything that had happened with my dad and with Toby, we had forgotten about it. I couldn't believe any stations had added my songs from it, but it was the only possibility that made sense. We asked if we could see which stations had listened to the songs and the service sent us a list of everyone who had downloaded my music for use.

The list included hundreds of stations. It was amazing. None of them were big markets, but there were hundreds of little stations, Internet stations, little one-man-show stations and they were all over the globe. I couldn't believe they'd even found the songs, let alone listened to them and added them to their playlists!

At the time I didn't know anything about radio promotion, but I knew those results couldn't be normal. Now that I've done this for a while, I know it was a miracle of God. Radio stations of any size normally have songs shopped to them by promoters who spend a lot of time just trying to get the music programmers to listen. Getting airplay is very difficult. I know this because I have a great promoter, and he has done a wonderful job for me over the years contacting the bigger stations and encouraging them to play my songs. Those stations are pretty much inaccessible in any other way.

The stations that were playing my songs were not, for the most part, those larger stations. They were smaller and more open to independent releases. But still, when you realize that there is an average of 300,000 albums released every year, you can imagine how many people are competing for attention and air time on any station. To have so many radio programmers stumble across my songs, take the time to listen, and then add them to their playlists was nothing short of miraculous! I knew God had done this.

God doesn't often let us stay in our comfort zones. I had always been a classical musician. And when I took my church job, I distinctly told them I would sing anything, but please, please, don't ask me to speak! Even though I had been singing my new music in concert with more frequency over the past months, it never would have occurred to me to really pursue contemporary music or seek out a speaking ministry. Now here I was, singing in a style I was not confident in, and sharing my story in front of audiences. God has a real sense of humor.

I think God knew I would never have thought of this path otherwise and He was telling me to pursue this ministry full time. We just needed to wait on Him to know how He would make it possible. With everything Toby was going through and raising our two girls as well, there wasn't a lot of time left over to pursue a new profession.

God knows us well. If He had let me continue in my chosen field, I would have taken the credit for any success I had. I worked very hard to be a classical musician and God knew that. Doing this new style of music, I could see that none of this was about me. Thankfully, my music training makes some of it easier, but I can't take credit for anything that has happened. It was all God's provision, and that keeps me trusting Him, relying on Him, and following Him.

In a very short period of time, God took away so many of the things upon which I had relied. He made me rethink assumptions and deal with issues of pride I hadn't even been aware that I had. My parents had always been my support and backup plan. Now my dad was gone and my mom was grieving. I had always been confident in my parenting. Now we knew that we couldn't help Toby ourselves, and while I needed to be faithful and do my best, God was ultimately in charge. God knew what Toby needed, and we could trust Him. In my music, God was taking those things I'd always counted on – my classical voice, performance style, and musical knowledge – and was throwing me in the deep end where I'd need a completely different skill set and voice. Truly, He was placing me where I would need to rely on Him alone.

People say to me, "How exciting that must have been with your music! That's so cool that it took off like that. It must have been a great time!"

In reality, it was scary. Classical music requires very specialized skills and classical vocal technique is a very particular way to sing. There are so many minute details of muscle use, posture, breathing, performance style, and musical interpretation. I had learned all the nuances of pronunciation for multiple languages and the correct historical musical interpretation for all of the major time periods and countries. I had taught music theory and practiced the piano until my fingers bled. I could write an eighteenth-century fugue or do a Roman numeral analysis of any piece. Only a few of those skills had any use in this new world. Was all that time wasted?

Now I needed to know all about technology and improvisation. I'd listen to other singers and hear how they used the microphone as a tool, and I became aware of all the minute details of this new art form that I'd never thought about or learned. Music had to come out of your head and no one was supplying the notes on paper. The playing style on the piano was new to me, and even rhythm was approached differently. Would I ever be good enough?

The stakes were high. It wasn't just a matter of pride. Any classical singer will tell you that you cannot deviate from your classical technique without consequences. So much depends on having your muscle memory in place so that, when you sing, your muscles remember exactly what they are supposed to do down to the tiniest detail. Singing in any other way confuses the muscles, causes potential damage to your vocal chords, and basically muddies your sound. Once you start singing in other ways, it's very hard to go back, so it's a choice to be made with your eyes open.

I already knew that I probably shouldn't be singing in this new style at church if I wanted to preserve my classical voice, but I felt that God wanted me there. I knew that pursuing this music full-time meant saying goodbye to my classical career. If I was to sing popular music all the time, I would never get that classical quality back to the level it had been. I had spent my life studying that way of singing, and I wanted to be very sure that I was supposed to change direction because there wasn't a way to reverse course. Even if I took the time to retrain myself, I knew opera companies and symphonies were not going to take me seriously after taking years off to pursue other things. It just isn't done.

I was also throwing myself into the ring with people who had sung this style their whole lives. My classical training was actually hurting me. I had to "unlearn" a lot of what I knew. Long vocal lines had to be chopped up. Pure pitches needed to be scooped. Precise diction meant to travel across a performance space had to be softened to prevent popping sounds through a microphone. Everything was different. This was a totally separate skill set, and while I was really prepared in a few areas, there were many more that were mystifying.

I was in a Bible study group around that time which involved watching a DVD lecture together. Soon after we received the news about the radio play for my songs, I went to my group with so many questions for the Lord. I was excited on one hand and terrified on the other. I was confused and really wanted clear direction. Why would God have had me pursue graduate work in classical music just to change direction now? Was I really hearing God or only listening for the answer I wanted? Was I just excited about the radio play? Did He want me to pursue this or pull back and be home full-time with my kids or even go back to teaching and the symphony?

I made a list of my questions. My thoughts were so chaotic; I had to give them order. That night I watched the lecture, and it is a night I will never forget. Point by point, the speaker addressed my questions in her videotaped lecture, some of them word for word. For example, I wrote, "Lord, I feel this might be a direction from You, but I am so scared to move forward. What if I haven't heard You correctly? You know how much is at stake and I don't want to make a mistake here." The speaker would say something like, "You might feel you have a direction from the Lord, but you are afraid to move forward. Maybe you're afraid you haven't heard Him right. You can trust God. You need to follow where He is leading." If it hadn't been so earth shattering for me, it would have been funny. God chose the lecture that night as a means to speak to me, and to reassure me of His direction. He knew I needed something specific, or I would have been paralyzed with fear.

God doesn't owe us answers, and He certainly doesn't owe us such specificity. But I feel strongly that when He shows His love for us by giving such a direct answer, we had better be willing to act on it. In my life, I can only point to a few times when I felt Him answer me so clearly. At other times, I feel His leading, but it's my responsibility to search His

Word, try to understand His character, and act in obedience to what I already know to be true from Scripture. In this case, He was gracious enough to confirm His message for me, and I knew that was where He was leading.

You would think that I would react with excitement and anticipation of what God would do. In reality, I cried the whole way home, and for the next few days after that. Don't get me wrong. I love my new ministry, and God has given me tremendous joy because of it that I never even thought was possible. I am truly blessed and I would not change anything now. But at the time, I knew I was closing the door on a career and an art form that had been a huge part of my life and make-up. There was a grieving process. There was a decision to be obedient. And then God gave me the excitement to look up and see what He would do with it.

CHAPTER 16

In the Classroom

December 2006

Toby's therapy became a huge part of our lives. We went four days a week to school, and I watched everything I could from the observation room, learning why the therapists did what they did. If I couldn't be there, Nathan would shift his work schedule and take Toby to class. Now that we understood more of the problem, it became fascinating to try to find ways to help Toby.

Because more people were understanding him, and he was gaining some means of communication, Toby's whole personality was changing. Gone was my sad, mad, frustrated, or even worse, shut down, silent child. He just blossomed. Toby has huge dimples, and he started smiling continuously. It wasn't until he started smiling so much that I realized how little he had smiled before. He was still very fearful of things, especially the unpredictable, but in therapy and at home where he understood the expectations and what was supposed to be happening, he gained such confidence. He finally had mastery over some parts of his world, and he was loving it!

One thing that was so touching was how the children in the class bonded. These eight little people clearly came to care for each other. If one of them fell down, another little guy would come over and pat him to make it all better. Often we would see a child get nervous about her mom or dad not being around and another child would take her hand and lead her over to knock on the observation window and gesture as if to say, "See? They're still there! No worries!" They would bring each other drinks and books. They were a wonderful group of kids.

I was also making friends with a lot of the parents in the observation room. Not everyone could stay, but many of us stayed at least some of the time, and we really got to know each other. This was such a wonderful godsend because it helped me to realize that I was not alone. Of the eight kids in the class, six of them were dealing with sensory issues to some degree. Toby was the most severe, but he also made the fastest gains in speech when they started addressing his sensory needs. We shared ideas about what had worked at home, what our kids were eating, or how someone found a great deal on the kind of t-shirts our kids could wear. That observation room had so many functions, and the support aspect was a really fun one. We even started setting up some play dates because the parents and children became so comfortable with each other.

One situation which started to arise in the classroom became pretty funny to us all. Most kids with SPD can be roughly grouped as either sensory seeking, where they need more sensory input and seek it out, or sensory avoiding, where they are too sensitive to input and avoid it whenever possible. We had kids in both camps in that class. Toby was very decidedly in the sensory avoidance group. He had one little friend named James* whom he loved so much. James was also a sensory avoider, and he and Toby would play by the hour, side by side, not touching, using clean wooden blocks or plastic toys, as happy as can be. They knew what to expect from each other, and neither of them was ever going to lean over and hug the other or be unpredictable.

On the other hand, Toby's other good buddy was a girl named Megan who absolutely loved touch. I don't know if she had any sensory issues, but she was certainly a hugger! Toby really liked her, and liked to play with her, but she made him so nervous! She was not predictable.

---

* The names of some children have been changed for reasons of privacy.

What would she do next? There was another boy, Joey, who was also a total sensory seeker, and often the four of them would play. We would laugh so hard (and then feel badly about it!) but it was really funny to watch Toby and James trying to keep everything all neat and predictable while Megan and Joey threw things and jumped on each other and hugged everyone.

One day I was sitting in the observation room for the OT gym with Megan, James, and Joey's moms, watching the class. Angie, the occupational therapist, had set up a new swing. It was a padded beam that the kids would straddle and it could swing four or five of them at once. Toby and James loved to swing, so they ran to it first and sat at opposite ends, perfectly happy. Then Megan and Joey saw them and ran to join them, Megan holding onto Toby for all she was worth, and Joey tightly hugging James. Toby and James' faces were priceless. Finally, Toby and James looked at each other, and with some sort of unspoken agreement, came to a plan. They stopped, got off the swing, pointed at Joey to move next to Megan and then got on together at the other end. Joey and Megan happily grabbed each other while James and Toby happily sat opposite them, not touching, and all of them swung away. It was a win-win situation for everyone.

Toby's math skills were also becoming more obvious. Every kid had a picture of themselves with a magnet on the back. At circle time, the teachers would call each child up and they would get to put their picture on the board. Then they would all count the pictures together to see how many children came to class that day. After that, if any of the children were missing they would count those pictures too.

One day in December there was a lot of sickness going around and three of the kids were missing. Toby was just over two years old at this point. There were already five pictures on the board and Stacey said, "Let's count! 1, 2, 3, 4, 5. Five friends at school today! I wonder how many are missing?"

Without missing a beat, Toby said, "Fwee."

Stacey did a double take and then said, "Toby, did you say three? But we haven't counted them yet!"

Toby answered, "Yes, fwee. No eight. Five. So fwee is bye-bye."

Stacey stared at him a second and then looked to the other teachers and said, "Did he just say that?" Then she laughed and said, "Toby, you are one smart cookie! You're right! Come up and help me count them now!"

Stacey came out after class and asked me if I'd seen that. I had. I was proud that Toby was smart, but in the back of my mind, I still wondered if this incredible gift with math could point to something on the autism spectrum. What he had just done was a kindergarten or first grade skill. Most two year old children are still trying to learn that a number can mean something, let alone count or do subtraction. So many things were improving for Toby, though, that I reminded myself of what my husband had said to me months ago. Maybe Toby was just good at math.

While Toby's speech was taking off, snack was not going as well. It was the one area he really struggled with and I had a lot of conversations with Angie about it. At this point, I was so frustrated with food. We had tried everything we knew, but Toby simply would not eat anything but his few standbys of dry Cheerios and Rice Krispies, round peanut butter crackers, milk and water. We started talking about food strategies. I hated to think what this very limited diet was doing to my son, especially since he was a baby and growing so fast.

When Toby was about fifteen months old, I had heard the old, "Just wait. When he gets hungry, he'll eat. You're babying him!" a few too many times, and I tried it. I didn't feed Toby any of his regular foods for a day and a half. I only offered him what we were eating, which is what I had done with the girls and it had worked beautifully. Instead of trying something new, though, Toby just didn't eat. He ate nothing. He was a fifteen month old baby who completely stopped eating. It wasn't stubbornness. I could tell several times that he wanted to eat but he couldn't. He would just cry when we tried to feed him. On the second day, I thought, "For goodness sake, he must be absolutely starving! Physically, it's not possible for him to not be hungry. We have to stop this!" I gave him dry Cheerios and he started sobbing in relief.

Since that day, I had been afraid to try to play hardball with food. Toby was trying to eat, he wanted to eat, but he couldn't do it. Sometimes he would watch us eat other foods and you could tell he wanted some, but it just wasn't possible for him. On the rare day we could get him to try something, he would often gag and cry as soon as it hit his tongue. We were giving him nutritional supplements, but we had to hold him down and squirt them down the back of his throat with a medicine dropper. He was so unhappy and so were we. It couldn't continue, but I was out of ideas. Our pediatrician and the ear, nose, and throat specialist had checked Toby's mouth and throat, and there were no structural or muscular problems.

Angie and Stacey sat down with me one day to discuss food strategies. We had realized since his diagnosis that, to Toby, most food was just intolerable in his mouth. Angie described it as "fingernails on a chalkboard. It's painful to him and he can't stand it. It makes him gag or hurts him so he refuses to let it in his mouth."

At the meeting Stacey said, "Basically, we are going to redefine baby steps for you. You are thinking that a baby step would be for Toby to take one bite of something. We are telling you that with his sensory issues and the fact that his mouth is the worst area for him, tasting something is about step twenty."

What had begun as a purely sensory problem for Toby was becoming behavioral. He was developing a phobia of food. Because his past experiences with food had been so negative, he was now avoiding it not just because it felt so bad in his mouth, but also because it was a habit to avoid it. We had to overcome all of that.

His teachers at school started by simply convincing Toby to stay seated with the class at snack time when there was food that was frightening to him on the table. This was most days since Toby was afraid of most foods. They would put a plate in the middle of the table and tell him it was his but he didn't have to touch it or have it near him. It would contain food that he didn't like and safe food as well, but he could just leave it in the middle of the table. Gradually, they moved the plate closer to him. They told him it was all his food and he owned it, but he didn't have to touch it or interact with it, he just had to let it be there. Eventually, he was able to tolerate having the plate in front of him.

Working through those steps took about three months. We copied this process at home, and even though Toby still wasn't eating anything but his standbys, he was able to sit at the table with us for five to ten minutes during meals rather than hiding in his red chair across the room. He often looked ready to run, and you could tell his anxiety was pretty high, especially when we started putting little bites of what we were eating on his plate. We would tell him it just had to sit there and he could eat his preferred foods. He would try so hard to cope, but the fight-or-flight response was undeniably still there.

The other side of it, though, was that Toby was so motivated to please us. Toby is the sweetest boy in the world, and he really wanted to make us happy. It was so touching to watch him sit there and try so hard for us. And as he had more success, and nothing terrible happened to him when the food was near him, he started to calm down. He wanted to be with us. He didn't want to be by himself in the red chair, and he started enjoying the family time. His occupational therapist, Angie, said our goal was to constantly push him farther without pushing him so far that he retreated due to fear.

I could see progress, but I won't lie, it was still frustrating. As it took months simply to sit at a table successfully, the dream of Toby actually eating nutritious food seemed to get farther and farther away. I wasn't looking forward to another holiday of explaining to extended family and friends why my son wouldn't eat their food and then listening to everyone's parenting advice. I knew they meant well, but it underscored the issues we were having and made me feel like people were judging us. The holidays were so much harder on Toby too with all the pressure to eat and all the strange foods, and I wanted to stay in our little therapy bubble at home.

It was so encouraging to see Toby's progress in speech, though. His vocabulary was exploding. Sometimes, it made me feel badly for the other parents at CSHC because not all of the children were responding to the therapy as quickly. I was still worried about Toby's other issues, but at least it had become clear that he was going to be able to communicate. It was becoming increasingly obvious that the CSHC program was exactly what he needed.

One realization just before Christmas break did temper my elation at Toby's progress in speech, though. I had been so excited about how well he was doing, and thought, "Yes! He's catching up! He's starting to use more two-word combinations, and he has so many words now. He'll be at age level before we know it!" I had it in my head that our goal was to get Toby up to the level he should have been at his intake at CSHC.

Then we spent more time with our extended families, and I saw how their two-year-olds were talking and suddenly it occurred to me — these kids were also gaining skills and developing. The goal line was moving. Toby was improving all the time, but the other children weren't waiting around for him to catch up! I know it seems silly not to have thought of that, but it really hadn't occurred to me. All of a sudden I realized that Toby didn't just have to develop on target, he had to make up for lost time. I hoped he could do it, and knew we would give him all the help we could.

CHAPTER 17

Working with Karen

Winter and Spring 2007

In January, we received word that a spot had opened up for Toby to
start private occupational therapy. We were going to be seeing Karen
Harpster. She quickly became a big part of our lives.

It was an adjustment for Toby to work with anyone new. He thrived
on predictability and loved that he knew all his teachers and all the kids
and the schedule every day at the school. We had tried to get him in with
Angie, the occupational therapist for the classroom, but she didn't have
any openings. We had heard rave reviews about Karen, but she had never
worked with a child with such severe feeding issues. In fact, there were
only one or two therapists at CSHC who really specialized in feeding and
they didn't have openings either.

We had looked into a few feeding therapy programs elsewhere, but
they made us really uncomfortable. We heard stories of children being
force fed or being told that their parents wouldn't come back until they
ate something. I couldn't imagine how holding a child down and forcing
food into his or her mouth would help overcome a phobia of food.
Wouldn't that make it worse? We liked the gentler approach we were
getting at CSHC, and it seemed that we would have better long-term
results even if the progress was slow. In every aspect of this process we
felt that God was giving us wisdom about what Toby needed. It was

important that we listened to Him and to our instincts about the best place for our child.

We met with Karen, and she told us that one of the occupational therapists at CSHC who was a food specialist was willing to mentor her and show her how to work with Toby. Karen was an excellent occupational therapist and willing to learn about food issues. She asked if we were comfortable with that arrangement. Since the alternative was waiting potentially another six months to a year for a spot with a food specialist and since Karen came highly recommended, we decided to give it a shot.

Karen did comprehensive testing on Toby in many areas. She had to modify some of the tests since he'd memorized a few of them from his previous testings. She confirmed his Sensory Processing Disorder diagnosis, but also gave us some unexpected news. In addition to SPD, Toby was delayed in his gross motor and fine motor development. He was testing above his age level for cognitive development and comprehension, but in all other areas, he was delayed.

Toby's motor actions were apparently another unexpected casualty of SPD. Since Toby's vestibular system made him feel continually off balance and he fell so frequently, he avoided movement. As a result, he hadn't developed his gross motor skills such as running, jumping, and throwing. Since he hated being messy or touching anything that wasn't plastic or wood, he didn't use his hands much and he certainly hadn't practiced using a fork. His hands were very weak and uncoordinated, and he hadn't developed his fine motor skills such as drawing or cutting or the skills needed for later schooling. He couldn't learn to dress himself because his hands were too weak to hold onto the clothes and his arms were too weak to pull them on. The sensory issues had some very far-reaching consequences.

It felt like the bad news just kept coming. Sensory Processing Disorder. Gross motor delay. Fine motor delay. Motor planning delay. Speech delay. Hearing impairment. Whenever we got comfortable with the idea that we were making progress, we seemed to find another problem. It was a roller coaster for Nathan and me. When was our little guy going to get a break?

Karen worked on each of these areas in private therapy. She also worked with me and taught me how to use our everyday lives as therapy for Toby. It was painful for me to watch him struggle to pull on his shirt, but I had to let him try. He wanted to do it himself, and he needed to do it. These problems were another vicious cycle, just like his phobia of food. When he didn't succeed, his sense of failure made him stop trying which in turn made him weaker and less able to succeed. We needed to find ways to break that cycle.

Karen told us that Toby really needed to learn to jump and walk on uneven surfaces. At two and a half, he still wouldn't walk over uneven ground without holding someone's hand, and he couldn't jump at all. We couldn't think of any way to have him practice jumping that would be safe. One day I saw a bounce house at a school function and thought it would be so perfect if they made a small one that could fit in our house. Then I found out, they do, although the small ones actually aren't very little. Ours was nine feet square, and it just barely fit in the playroom in our basement. Toby would go down there with Rinnah and Rachel and play for hours. It was perfect for him because he had to practice balancing the whole time, but falling never hurt. It also made us the coolest house on the block when friends came over!

Toby loved his therapy, but it was hard work. Karen would make him exercise his muscles so he would gain strength. They would set up obstacle courses and do a "wheelbarrow" with Karen holding Toby's legs as the handles and Toby walking on his hands. Because Toby loved puzzles, Karen would put a puzzle on one side of the room and the pieces on the other and put Toby face down in a hammock swing. He'd have to pick up a piece and then swing and drop it next to the puzzle board and when he had them all, he could solve it. It made him practice motor planning, while also holding his head up when face down which was really hard for him with his weak muscles. The swinging helped his vestibular system.

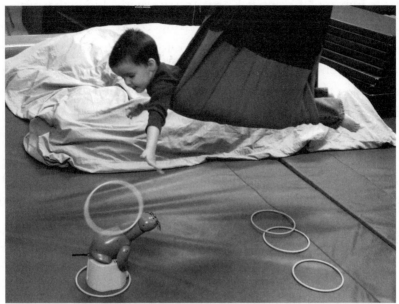

The hammock swing in the OT gym

After they did large muscle work, they would work on fine motor skills. Often, they would combine the tasks with sensory therapies as well. Toby hated for things to be messy, and one of the more brilliant things Karen did to capitalize on this was to play "car wash" with little toy cars. Toby couldn't stand to touch anything messy, so one of her goals was to get him to touch shaving cream without fear. She would "drive" the cars through a pile of shaving cream, and Toby could then "drive" them to the car wash: a dish of water. He could make the cars clean again which he loved! It was often enough motivation to get him to touch the messy cars for a moment, although he would need to wash his hands immediately.

The last ten or fifteen minutes of each session focused on food. Toby would have a picnic with Karen. I didn't care for some of the more common therapeutic foods. Why should we work really hard to get Toby to eat a gummy fruit snack that had no nutritional value? Or a marshmallow or a piece of cake? Some of those were great for sensory problems, but surely there were appropriate sensory foods that were good for him too! I wanted Karen to stick with things that we needed immediately. We really hoped that Toby could stop taking so many supplements, and he needed nutritious food to do that. Nathan and I talked to Karen about it, and she concentrated on yogurt, cheddar cheese, apples, and baby carrots. I desperately wanted Toby to have some source of protein and at least one vegetable.

That spring Toby made a lot more progress in the area of food, but it was still agonizingly slow. We all worked on it in parallel, his teachers in class, Karen in private therapy, and our family at home. Toby was accepting food on his plate, and could now stir or touch it with a popsicle stick. Next, his therapists encouraged him to "kiss the stick goodbye" when he threw away his trash. He'd do that sometimes, although many times he would physically shudder.

Eventually they would ask him to touch the end of his tongue to a food, just to taste it. That way he didn't have to commit to having it in his mouth and he could get used to the sensation of the flavor. We still use this technique a bit to this day since it relieves his anxiety about how something will feel and taste before he has to take an entire bite of it.

Karen started to keep a list of foods that Toby had managed to touch to his tongue or taste. The goal was ten foods. When Toby reached that goal, Karen told him they would have a party. Toby was so excited! He talked about it often, and when they finally reached that milestone, he was thrilled! Then he asked what kind of party they were going to have. Karen told him she would make a cake for him! As Toby's face fell, we all remembered that Toby hated cake. He couldn't handle the texture and the frosting made him shudder. Talk about demotivating!

Karen just laughed and said, "Toby, what a silly I am. Of course you don't want a cake! We're going to have Cheerios and graham crackers and play with lots of puzzles!"

Toby laughed with her and said, "Dat's good! Fanks."

We did have some breakthroughs with food that spring, though, and it really helped my stress level about Toby's nutrition. The first was that while Toby couldn't stand the texture of bread, he was willing to eat little bits of toast. I tried putting peanut butter on it and cutting it in little bites he could eat with a fork since he would never have been able to touch something like that with his hands. He actually liked it! We had a food with wheat bread and a protein! I felt like having my own party!

It was still hard to handle eating food away from home. I couldn't take a toaster with me. I found that Toby was also willing to eat my pancakes. He wouldn't eat any other kind, but he would let me bring some along from home. I discovered the joys of white whole wheat flour (just as nutritious as regular whole wheat, but with a much subtler flavor), and made endless batches of whole wheat pancakes. We'd make peanut butter sandwiches out of them and they became a nutritious travel food. It was pretty incredible!

Karen encouraged Toby to try apples and he discovered he liked them as long as they were peeled and sliced. He didn't have the jaw strength to bite a whole apple anyway. He hadn't spent a lot of time chewing in his life. She could also coax him to eat a baby carrot every once in a while, but they weren't his favorite. Karen continued to work at adding yogurt and cheese every week, and he finally ate those after about six months, although never in large amounts.

Another favorite food was banana muffins. It puzzled us that Toby loved banana muffins and pancakes, but the texture of regular bread would make him gag. We weren't going to argue, though. I'd make the banana muffins with applesauce and white whole wheat flour to make them more nutritious. At the end of February, one of his first long sentences was, "Dat's a goo' nana fuffin, mama!" Our whole family started calling them "nana fuffins."

Eventually we convinced him to eat bananas with peanut butter spread on them. I really felt we had a whole new world opening up to us. It sounds silly to get so excited about a few foods, but it changed everything. His only protein was peanut butter, and he still didn't have any vegetables, but he was starting to eat things from all the food groups, and I saw light at the end of the tunnel. Now, instead of four foods, we had over ten!

Every morning he would eat dry cereal, but he would also have a glass of milk with it. Why should I care if he ate them together or separately? For lunch and dinner he would have either a peanut butter banana, peanut butter toast, or a peanut butter pancake with apple slices and an occasional carrot. Every once in a while we'd give him a "nana fuffin" instead, and if he was feeling really adventurous, a few bites of cheddar cheese.

His therapists advised us to try to "normalize" his food more. Since his foods were so limited, we had fallen into the habit of making the family food and then making Toby his own separate meal. The therapists suggested that we have everything on everyone's plate, whether we ate it or not, so that Toby got the idea that all this food was just food, not Toby's food versus everyone else's food. So we started having our whole family put at least a bite of everything on their plates. Toby would just let his sit there, but that was a major milestone in and of itself. I was so proud of Rinnah and Rachel because they were such great sports about it. They thought it was strange, but they wanted to help Toby. I remember one night I had on my plate a piece of fish, green beans, watermelon, a small peanut butter pancake, apple slices, a graham cracker, and a dab of yogurt. Not a typical combination, but that was our family.

The foods Toby would actually eat were still very limited, but the real miracle was that he was sitting with us. He was enjoying meals with us and he wasn't scared of his food. He became more and more comfortable, and he started to feel that it was normal to sit at a table and enjoy eating and being with his family. The stress level went down significantly, although I frequently still had to feed him. Somehow he could handle eating the food, but if he also had to touch it with his hands, the experience became overwhelming. He couldn't stand having his hands messy, and his fine motor skills made it very hard for him to use a fork without getting frustrated. I would often put the food on the fork for him and then let him put it in his mouth to encourage him to interact with the food a bit more.

Toby also discovered a love for chocolate during this time, specifically M&M's and plain milk chocolate. Clearly, he was related to me! This became important because, as everyone knows, chocolate can be a powerful motivator. Toby would try almost anything for an M&M! We definitely took advantage of this in therapy.

Often I would get frustrated about Toby's eating. There were many days when I wished we could simply sit at the table and eat a meal without it involving Nathan and I both continuously monitoring and encouraging just one more touch or taste of something. Sometimes it was too much and I would try not to cry while we were clearing the table. We had not had a stress-free family meal in Toby's lifetime.

At these times, I would remind myself of what God had already done in Toby's life. God had given us hope, and He gave us more each day. Toby might not eat without a struggle, but he was eating. Toby might not be able to touch his food, but he could talk to us about it now. We might not be able to enjoy mealtimes, but it was clear that he was improving and we were going to be able to interact with and enjoy Toby for the rest of his life. We could be thankful about so many things.

CHAPTER 18

Transitions

Spring 2007

E ven with all the progress we were seeing, I was still worried about Toby's prognosis. It seemed that every time we thought we had a handle on the problem, we received more bad news. Generally, autism is not diagnosed in children younger than age three, although that is changing, so I was never able to banish that fear completely. Was SPD the complete answer? Or was something else coming?

At age three, all children in the county special needs program move to the corresponding special needs program in their school district and must be re-tested to qualify for services. This would happen for Toby in the coming fall. There is a formal process to make the transition with many meetings beforehand and we began the process that spring. At one of these meetings with Toby's therapists, I asked if there was any concern in their minds that Toby might be autistic.

"Ah, you're going to bring out the big A-word, huh?" our speech therapist, Stacey, asked. "You know, that's the fear for a lot of parents, and of course you should speak to his pediatrician if you're concerned. I'm not going to rule it out because he's so young, but I'm not particularly worried about it for him either. He's making beautiful progress here, and the occupational therapy seems to be addressing the issues correctly for him. You're doing everything you can."

I responded, "So you're saying that we should just wait and see."

Stacey replied, "Yes, but I'm also saying that even if it is autism, his current therapies would be what he would need anyway, so you're doing the right thing. And I do feel that SPD is going to be the final diagnosis for Toby."

That was reassuring, but certainly not definitive. One thing I have learned over the years is that God rarely lets us know His plans in advance. We have to trust Him for each step. I like to be in control, but sometimes life circumstances strip away the illusion of control that we all try to maintain. We are never really in control but it's scary to be forced to admit it. We do know, however, that God is good. Nathan and I had to give the situation to God every day and trust Him to take care of our son and his future.

By the end of that spring, Toby's speech had made incredible gains. He was quickly catching up to his peers in that area, and his personality was blossoming. As he was able to communicate more effectively, his confidence grew.

I remember one day that made me laugh hysterically. We have a small family room and Toby and Rinnah and Rachel were all in it, and I was sitting nearby. All of a sudden, Toby decided he needed to release some energy, and he yelled out at the top of his lungs, "Wook out, my sistews! I is gonna wun awound now!!" And he proceeded to run as fast as he could in circles while the girls dove onto the couches, laughing.

His delivery made us smile, but in truth, it was almost unbelievable to see his progress in only eight months. This child who didn't speak or smile or move or interact without tears in September was now racing around, being silly on purpose to make his sisters laugh, and telling them what he was doing in full sentences! It was miraculous, and that day my heart felt ready to burst with the hope I was feeling.

We certainly weren't done. Toby had been exposed to hundreds of foods that year and could only eat about ten. At the end of his school year at CSHC, the therapists said the severity of his food aversion made it a medical condition that needed to be addressed by our doctor in addition to his occupational therapist. Toby still only had one kind of shirt he could tolerate, and he would touch almost nothing. He also had a severe fine motor delay and he couldn't step off curbs or go up and down stairs because of his vestibular system. He didn't know how to jump or catch a ball or peddle a tricycle. But he was so happy, and his beautiful, dimpled smile was shining out almost constantly.

We continued to worry about him, but now the nature of our concerns had changed. At the beginning of the year, I had worried Toby would never communicate, that he would never be able to love someone outside of our family or leave our home, that he would never eat and would need a feeding tube. Now I knew none of those things were going to be his reality. We saw so much progress, and as the bigger issues improved, we could concentrate on smaller ones.

During this time, we were experiencing some difficulties with our girls. Toby was taking so much of our energy and attention. There were times when Rinnah and Rachel felt pushed aside or ignored, and they were sometimes jealous. This is such a common problem in families with special needs kids and typical siblings. It's hard for a child to see the benefits of being typical when they see their sibling getting so much additional attention.

We discussed these things frequently with the girls, and, while it was difficult, for the most part they understood. Rinnah and Rachel loved Toby and were very supportive of him. Nathan and I just needed to

typical

the term used in the special needs community to describe a child who is developing in a typical way, that is, without special needs

typical peer

a student meant to provide a model of age-appropriate skills in a special needs classroom make sure the girls knew we loved and cherished them every bit as much as we loved their brother. It grieved us both to think that our precious daughters were hurting, and we wanted them to know how proud we were of them and how special they were to us. We made a concerted effort to spend more time with them one on one which helped a lot.

At the end of the school year, we had a huge decision to make about how to handle Toby's therapy during the summer. The CSHC program ended in the spring. If Toby qualified through the school district, that program wouldn't start until the fall. CSHC had a summer option which was excellent, but it wasn't covered by the county or by our insurance and it was very expensive. I hated the idea of Toby going three or four months without the intensive therapy school had given him.

To make it harder, Toby was going to have to do all of his evaluations again at the end of the summer when he transitioned to the school district. SPD was not considered a primary delay at the time which meant that you couldn't qualify for special education services with SPD alone. To qualify for services, a child needs to test two standard deviations below the mean in one primary area, or one and a half standard deviations below the mean in two primary areas. The areas which qualified were speech delay, gross motor delay, fine motor delay, and many other areas in which Toby was totally typical and would not qualify. We knew that if he continued the progress he was making through the summer, he was not likely to qualify for services, which

primary delay

an area of delay which is significant enough to qualify a child for special education services through a school district

For instance, cognitive impairment, speech and language impairment, or specific learning disabilities are all examples of possible primary delays.

would mean we would have to pay for them out-of-pocket. If we didn't do the summer program, he would probably lose ground, but he would also be more likely to qualify for special education services which would get us three free years of therapeutic preschool.

I hate to admit that I would ever make decisions about my child's care because of money, but it's a serious consideration for almost every parent of a special needs child. It seemed so ironic that if we chose to pay for the expensive therapy Toby needed, it would probably cost us three years of free support, and if we didn't, we could get the rest of his preschool paid for. I knew Toby would be right on the borderline of qualifying, and the summer therapy could easily tip the balance.

People said to us, "Well, wouldn't it be great if he didn't qualify? That would mean he was better! He wouldn't need the help anymore!" That sounds correct, but in reality, only about the lowest three to five percent of children qualify for help, and the only reason Toby was borderline at this point was because of all the interventions he was receiving. We knew he was going to continue to need that help. And if our child was disqualified because he happened to be in the lowest four percent rather than the lowest three percent, it would not be very comforting.

In the end, we decided to sign Toby up for the summer program and trust God to help us know what should be done in the fall. Everything that I had read about early intervention testified to the importance of getting as much help as possible before the age of three. These were our last few months in that window, and I didn't want to waste them. We also put Toby on the wait list to be a typical peer at the district special needs preschool. We figured that way, if he didn't qualify, he could still attend the school even though we would have to pay for it and he wouldn't get any extra help. At least he'd have teachers who had experience with SPD and would understand how to deal with his issues and be able to teach him effectively.

CHAPTER 19

Back to the Beach

May and June 2007

D uring the previous school year, I had done some singing here and there. There had been very little at the beginning. I was really depressed after Dad died, and between that, Toby's therapy, the girls' schooling, and my job at the church, I really had more than I could handle. I knew God was leading us into this music ministry, but He also knew I didn't know how to pursue it, so we just did the best we could and waited for Him to lead us.

I didn't have much time to seek out events, so I accepted invitations when I could, but I didn't look for anything more. My mom often came with me, and it was helpful for her to see our family's story used for something good. She also had a great ministry of her own. When audiences heard that my mom was with me, often people who had also lost a loved one or had been through a personal tragedy would come and talk with her. She has a real gift for sharing God's faithfulness with people.

After the term ended at CSHC that spring, I had a larger tour planned. I was getting better at coordinating events and was headed down to Florida to sing at several churches. Nathan and I decided to make it a family trip and take the kids. There were a few free days between concerts and we thought we'd have some time together before Toby's summer therapy began.

One of the churches I was visiting offered to put us up in a member's beach house in St. Augustine for a few days. Usually, a church will cover my hotel stays, but I had never had an offer like this! The member was just so pleased that we were coming, and wanted us to enjoy it.

Before we had Toby, I would have been thrilled! What a wonderful gift and opportunity! But given our experience last fall at the beach, I was suddenly terrified. I did not want to go back to the beach. I'd been clinging to this fragile idea that everything was fine now. Toby was improving every day. His speech was better and he was eating. I could pretend that we were just like everyone else.

The truth was that everything wasn't okay. I couldn't imagine that Toby could handle a beach. I was still grieving my dad terribly, and the past year with Toby had been grueling. I was so sick of being sad all the time. I felt like Nathan was carrying the load for me so often because I was depressed or overwhelmed. Concentrating on our girls and on getting Toby what he needed had been all that had kept me going.

Going back to the beach would just highlight all the things Toby couldn't do. I didn't want to face the problems he might have or watch him struggle with something that everyone else enjoyed. It would be too hard, and I just wanted to avoid it. But how could we say, "No, thank you. That's one of the nicest offers we've ever received, but we'd much rather just stay at a hotel." I didn't want to have to explain it, and it was so kind of them that there was no easy way to turn it down.

We accepted their offer. I was a little angry with God for putting us in this position. Didn't He know how hard it would be? But then I felt so ungrateful for being mad about a free beach house! I gave myself a good talking-to, and told myself how much the girls would love it. Nathan could play with them and Toby and I would hang out inside the whole time if needed. We would be fine!

When we arrived, we found ourselves in a cute little condo about a hundred steps from the beach. It was pretty great, really. We decided to take a walk around before lunch. Toby was fine to come with us, but he didn't want to walk on all that sandy, uneven ground. No problem – it was close and we could carry him. When we got outside, Toby looked concerned. It wasn't windy, though, and we told him we weren't going to get wet. We were just going to look around a little before we ate. He relaxed against Nathan's shoulder and enjoyed the walk.

As Nathan and I stood at the edge of the dunes and looked out at the water, we realized this was the perfect beach. If an occupational therapist had designed a therapeutic beach for a kid with SPD, this would have been it. It was wide and flat with little tidal pools everywhere where a child could play and get wet without worrying about waves. Most of the beach was hard-packed sand, so the footing was solid, and the sand was wet so it was cool to the touch and didn't blow around. It was calm with very little wind, and small waves lapped gently at the shore. It was even the perfect temperature that day, not too hot and not too cold.

We went back to the condo to eat lunch and afterward I put Toby down for a nap. Nathan knew what I was thinking even though I hadn't said anything. He knew I was afraid of the emotions connected to this environment, and he needed to push me a little. He said, "When Toby wakes up, I think we should try it. We'll take it slow. I think it would be good to try." He helped the girls get ready for the beach and they headed out.

I knew Nathan was right, so when Toby woke up, he and I put on swimsuits and went to find Nathan and the girls. I carried Toby over the dunes and across the dry sand until we were on the hard, flat, wet sand. He was a little nervous, but he wasn't crying. I stood there holding him and we watched his sisters play. I thought it was a miracle that we were there. After a while, I realized Toby was happy to be with his family and content to watch his sisters playing in the waves.

Slowly, I set his bare feet down on the hard-packed sand. He stared down at his toes and wiggled them and I held my breath, sure that he would cry. He didn't. He just looked serious and stayed there, wriggling his toes in the sand. Over the next hour and a half, we moved so slowly, so gently, getting him acclimated to standing on the sand, then touching his toes to the water in the tidal pools. Eventually, he stood at the edge of one and splashed his toes in it a bit, even touching it twice with his fingertips. Then we walked to the edge of the ocean to watch his dad and sisters in the waves.

Rachel with Toby, testing the sand

I coaxed him out a bit at a time until the water lapped his toes and I thought what a miracle I was witnessing. Then, unexpectedly, a bigger wave came, splashing him all the way to his knees, and I turned to snatch him up out of the water, expecting to find that the work of the last hour and a half had just been destroyed by that wave. But instead of crying, I heard Toby laughing. I looked down at his face to see him smiling with such surprised joy. He exclaimed, "I have fun! Mama, I have fun!"

Instantly I was crying on the beach again. Not only because I had seen such a miracle with my son that day, but because God loved me so much that He forced me to go back to the beach and see what He had done for Toby. The words of Revelation 21 came to me: "He who was seated on the throne said, 'I am making everything new!'" It was as if

God was giving me a foretaste of what He wanted for all of us – healing and life the way it was meant to be.

Nathan and the girls saw us by the water and came back in to play by Toby. We all made a huge sandcastle, Toby helping occasionally by pressing some sand in with his toes. He wouldn't touch it with his hands yet, but even so, he got some sand on them and he didn't panic, he just asked me to brush them off. He wanted to stay with us more than he wanted to go home and clean his hands.

Over the next two days, Toby learned to love the beach. It was such a gift. Nathan and I laughed at how much therapy this time on the beach was! Our whole life seemed like therapy at that point, but this was fun for everyone. Later that summer we went to another beach with extended family and Toby actually asked Nathan to take him into the waves and even learned to make sandcastles by himself. He still couldn't sit on the sand or touch it, but he would sit on our laps and use a shovel, and he had a great time. He could play with his family and all the other children! It was miraculous.

Even while we were overwhelmed with this amazing breakthrough at the beach, there were still issues. We could never get completely comfortable because some days were good and some weren't and Toby was still unpredictable. He continued to have strong clothing preferences. We had found a t-shirt the previous year which had no stitching or designs of any kind, and when he tried it out and was able to wear it, I went and bought it in every color. It was all he wore. That store seemed to bring out something similar every year, though, so the shirt issue wasn't too difficult. I just bought them in a bigger size and it wasn't very hard to get Toby to switch.

Shoes were a different story, though. Toby had only been able to wear one pair of shoes for the entire year and they were far too small by that spring. One would think that with his sensory issues he would want new shoes, but he was completely attached to them and terrified to change. I bought him a pair of sandals and started trying to transition him for the summer. It was ridiculous. We worked at it like we worked at food, first putting them close to his feet, then touching his feet, then putting them on for ten seconds, thirty seconds, a minute. It was so frustrating. I just wanted to change his shoes, already!

Finally, in mid-June after six weeks of trying to change his shoes, we were at a summer open house for Rachel's preschool. Nathan had taken the girls to get ice cream. They'd been gone for over twenty minutes and I was still in the car trying to get Toby to wear his shoes. His old ones had finally fallen apart and I was at the end of my patience. He needed to do this! I put them on and he started to cry. We climbed out of the car and I carried him into the open house where he continued to cry about those shoes for the next fifteen minutes. It felt as if everyone was staring at us before he calmed down. He was just barely holding it together, but he finally did it. I couldn't set him down because he couldn't walk in the new shoes, but he left them on his feet. We went home and I cried again. How in the world were we going to keep doing this? Why was it so hard? How was a person supposed to grow up and function if they couldn't even change their shoes?

It was a constant roller coaster of emotions, one day so happy with Toby's progress and the next one just wondering how we could get through one more day. There were so many times I just wanted to give up. I was so tired of everything being a battle and being on edge all the time. I wanted to sit down and eat a meal and not think about all the ramifications. I wanted to go somewhere and not worry about the weather or his clothes or whether people would think my son was cute and try to touch him.

The truth is that for parents of special needs kids, there are no days off. Parents are their child's most effective advocate, and no one else will take up the fight for their child in the same way. Toby himself was our best encouragement. We loved him so much. He was such a wonderful kid, and when I saw joy on his face, it was the best motivation God could ever give me to keep fighting.

CHAPTER 20

Finding Beauty

Summer 2007

That summer, several things were going on with my music. I was getting more invitations to sing and speak, and I was part of a small regional tour of independent artists. We went to different churches and festivals in the Midwest and each group or artist would play about twenty minutes. I was also writing new songs. There were so many things going on in my life, and many of them found their way into my lyrics.

Ever since we had heard about the radio play for my first album, I had wondered what we could accomplish on the radio if we really tried to produce songs at radio quality. I called Jon from Workbook Studio, and asked him what he thought I should do. We felt like God had confirmed this new ministry and He was already using it, but we didn't know how to proceed. Jon had a lot more contacts than we did and a lot more knowledge of how the industry worked.

I had written enough songs for a second album at this point. Jon said we should take a couple of the new songs and produce them to the highest standard we could, and then shop them around as singles to try to get more mainstream airplay. He was amazed by the radio play I had received from the first album, and was happy for me. We also talked about recording the entire album over the summer and fall.

Nathan and I prayed a lot about it. It was a big financial step and a commitment to the ministry. Since I didn't have a label, we had to come up with the money ourselves, and we knew we'd have to sell a lot of CDs to pay for a project this ambitious. In the end, we both felt it was the right thing to do, and I started thinking about which songs would be the first to be produced.

The first songs we concentrated on were "Hands to the Sky" and "Beauty from Pain." I had written "Beauty from Pain" earlier in the year, and it was especially close to my heart. It was based on Isaiah 61:3 which says God will "bestow on them a crown of beauty instead of ashes." When I had first read Isaiah 61 the previous fall, that verse just struck me and then stayed with me. At that time, I saw so many ashes everywhere in my life, and I started to pray that God would show me the beauty that would come from them.

God answered that prayer in so many ways. He started opening my eyes to the beautiful things that He had done through my dad while Dad was sick. So many people met the Lord through my dad's story and blog. God showed me how he had changed my family as we had all become united in one cause during Dad's illness. And He showed me all of the things He was doing for Toby. Toby was just such a source of beauty and joy. We still had a lot of fears and questions, but no one could deny the miracle of change that we saw in him.

Most of all, God showed me how my faith had deepened. That previous year with Toby's deterioration, Dad's death, Toby's diagnosis, the whirlwind of information and therapy, the unexpected reception of my songs, and a complete career change had swept away almost everything I had ever stood on as a foundation. I had needed to cling to God in a way I never would have if things had been going well. There are so many wonderful promises in the Bible. God will not leave you or forsake you (Deuteronomy 31:8). God will use all things to good for those who love Him (Romans 8:28). God is our refuge and strength and an ever-present help in trouble (Psalm 46:1). All of these promises were my lifeline, and God was absolutely trustworthy for each one. His faithfulness took my breath away. It changed my understanding of God in ways that I never thought possible, and that was such a thing of beauty. Even with all the pain of the past year, I would never have traded what I learned through it.

I decided to name the album *Finding Beauty* after Isaiah 61. I wanted the album to help people, so I put every Scripture that I used to write the songs into the liner notes so people could find them if they needed them. I included many personal songs which had been written during the past year. They were my cries to God in my darkest hours, and my praises to Him for His faithfulness. "Godspeed" was from Dad's funeral. "Hands to the Sky" was about totally surrendering to God's will. "We'll Be Together" was a song for my mom affirming that she would see my dad again. "Higher" was about praising God in every situation. "Want to Be Found" was about seeking God even in my darkest depression. "Give Me Jesus" was my dad's favorite hymn, so I wrote an arrangement of it.

Recording *Finding Beauty*

I even wrote a song for Toby. I called it "Hello, Sunshine" because of his smile. Toby has the most amazing dimples and when he smiles, it's like the sun coming out. We had only seen that smile a few times in his young life, but as he started therapy, we watched it begin to shine. He hardly ever stopped smiling now. Everything had changed for him, and it felt like he was becoming the little boy he had always been inside but had been unable to express. I dedicated the song to the staff at CSHC.

This time we recorded the songs in Jon's new studio and spent a lot more time and money to get the songs to the level we wanted. We knew the production value needed to be significantly higher than it had been on the first album if we were going to have a chance to get on bigger radio stations. I also knew I'd have to find a radio promoter. We weren't going to get on the stations that determined the national charts by listing it for $30 as we had before.

Rinnah and Rachel, helping in the studio

I had no idea how to find a radio promoter. Many people believe that getting a song played on the radio is like something out of the movie *Coal Miner's Daughter* where I could just drive around to radio stations and hand them the CD, or email them and they'd listen and add the song. In reality, it's nearly impossible to get a large market station to even listen to a song without some kind of promoter or personal connection. One of the problems with changing careers so completely was that now I had no idea what I was doing, and no connections to help me do it. Jon's promoter didn't do Christian music so he didn't know people at the right stations. Neither Jon nor his promoter knew of any promoters for Christian music. There were a lot of "radio promotion services" out there, but from what I could see, they just cost a lot of money, and wouldn't really do much for an artist like me.

Here I was again with a problem and no idea how to solve it. God had been so faithful to us with Toby's therapy. We hadn't known where to turn, and yet He ordered our steps and opened doors and led us through the whole process. We knew He was leading this ministry. Why would I not trust that He would also provide what we needed now?

I got down on my knees and prayed about it for a long time. "Lord, You know I need a radio promoter. You know I need an honest one who will not cost me a million dollars and will actually get the music where it needs to be. You know I can't just look this up. I think You want me to pursue this, and if You do, I need You to provide me with a promoter. If I'm wrong about this, let me know. I want Your will in it. But if You want me to pursue this, please tell me how."

I got up when I finished praying and went to check my email. I had a message from a friend, Chris, in North Dakota whom I'd met when she booked me to do a show out there. She had booked some other artists over time and kept up with them as well. I hadn't told her I was looking for a promoter, but her message said, "You know, I was thinking you should ask Ginger Millermon which radio promoter she uses. You'd be on similar stations, and I'm sure she'd love to help."

Ginger Millermon is another independent Christian artist. I'd seen her music several places and she'd had a number of songs chart nationally on Christian radio. I had never talked to her. Why in the world would she help me? And what was I supposed to do, just call her up and say, "Hey, Ginger, you've never heard of me, but this lady in North Dakota said you might help me?"

Well, why not? I've learned to care a lot less about looking stupid. And really, when you ask God for direction, and you get a lead, you should probably follow it!

Chris had sent me Ginger's phone number, and I called her, never thinking she'd answer. She answered after the second ring and was completely helpful and pleasant, never sounding like it was the least bit odd to have some stranger call her and ask about her business practice. We were only on the phone for about three minutes, but she said, "You need Wendell Gafford. If he says he'll take a song, it's because he believes you will get play. He's honest, and he knows everyone. I have no idea if he'll take you, but if he does, he will get you on the radio."

Wow. Here I had prayed for direction and less than fifteen minutes later I had a name. Another miracle! I have a hard time calling people I don't know and asking for help, so I called Wendell right away before I lost my courage. He also answered after the second ring. God wasn't going to give me a chance to back out before I'd talked to these people!

I told him my story, and he was extremely nice, but just as nicely he told me he didn't have time for me.

"Please," I said, "Could you just listen to the project? Or some of it? I can send you a couple of singles."

"No, I'm sorry, I really can't. I have no time right now and I can't take on a new artist."

"Please, just listen to it before you decide. Please?"

"If I listen to it, I'm going to charge you for my time. Not because I'm trying to take your money, but because I need to know you're serious. I have no time and you have no idea how often I'm asked to do this. And I'm going to tell you up front that I'm probably not going to take you."

"That's okay. I understand, but I'd really like you to hear it before you decide."

So I emailed him the project and wondered if I'd hear from him again. He called me back three days later and said, "Jennifer, I was really hoping you'd be bad because I really don't have time for this. But it's good and I think you could get some airplay with it. If you can wait for three months, I will take it then."

I was ecstatic because the project wasn't really going to be ready to release until late fall or winter anyway. It was perfect! Over the years, I've had numerous radio programmers tell me that Wendell was the reason that they listened to me in the first place. I've heard how he only sends good songs to them, and how he understands their stations and the kind of music they are looking for. He loves the Lord, and wants to help artists' ministries by getting their music out there. He's become a friend, and I can never deny that it was God who connected us.

CHAPTER 21

Another New Beginning

August 2007

B y the end of the summer, Toby had made a lot more progress. His time in the summer program at CSHC had really helped. His speech was great by now, although he continued to have some articulation issues since his mouth was still a little uncoordinated. His gross motor skills were improving, and he was able to deal with change and new situations with greater confidence. With all that said, we were sure he still needed help, and we were facing the testing to see if Toby would qualify as a special needs child in our school district.

This testing was different because in the federal program for ages zero to three, the focus is on all developmental delays. That is a very broad net, and covers the entire scope of things that could affect a child before age three. When children transition to the school district, though, the definition of "special needs" becomes much narrower. A child can qualify for services only if his impairment affects his ability to learn in school. A fine motor delay means a child can't hold his pencil correctly to learn to write so it qualifies. Not being able to eat food or touch sand · does not.

SPD is being debated everywhere at the time of the writing of this book. At the time of our testing, it was considered a secondary condition, meaning that if you qualified in another area but also had

SPD, they would address both. But SPD by itself was not a qualifying problem. I knew Toby would never qualify at this point for speech delay so the question to be determined was if he would still have a severe enough delay in his gross motor and/or fine motor skills to qualify.

The first time Toby willingly approached water

The teachers at CSHC told me to be prepared because they did not expect him to qualify. Most special needs preschool programs have very low thresholds for qualification, and, by this time, Toby had made tremendous progress. Everyone felt that he would just miss it. But, I was given a glimmer of hope because our school district was considered forward thinking and proactive in this area. They believed it was better to put time and energy into helping preschoolers catch up and be successful from the beginning than to wait until the children were in real trouble at a later age and try to help them then.

As we got ready for testing, I had several people ask me why I wanted my child to be labeled as a special needs child. Was it just the free preschool? Did I want the attention? Shouldn't it make me happy to know my child didn't qualify for special needs services anymore?

The answers to those questions were complicated. Of course we would be happy if Toby didn't need special education services, but the truth was that whether Toby qualified for services or not, he needed them. The only reason he was borderline at this point was because he had eleven to twelve hours a week of formal therapy and constant support at home. I knew if we stopped all that, he'd never continue to make the progress we were seeing. If he didn't qualify, we were just going to have to find some way to pay for it all. So, yes, free therapeutic preschool was a big part of it.

The other side of it was that the label had never bothered me much. Call him whatever you need to call him to get him help. I know people do not want to label their children. They are afraid of what others will think or how they will react to their child because of that label. But what people seem to miss is that their child will be labeled one way or another no matter what they do. You can choose to give their teachers a label such as "SPD" or "speech delayed" that helps the teacher to understand your child's behavior and react in a way that's helpful, or you can ignore it and wait until they are labeled as "aloof," "uncooperative," "unintelligent," "unfriendly," "out of control," or "difficult." Or worse, wait until they get labels that are completely incorrect and have far-reaching consequences. Many kids with SPD are wrongly diagnosed as having ADHD or emotional problems or depression, and treated medically for those issues. I hate the idea of those young brains on medications for conditions they may not even have!

Also, when children are young, they don't know they have a label. Toby had no idea that he was a "child with SPD." Why would I choose to reject this label now, when accepting it would get Toby the help he needed and possibly free him of a label later? My choosing whether or not to acknowledge that Toby had issues did not change the fact that they were there.

I have seen many parents struggle with this over the years we have spent in special needs programs and schools. I have seen parents decide to send their child to a neighborhood preschool, determined that everything will be fine even after being told that their child needs support. They cling to the idea that if they pretend everything is okay, it will be. But, truthfully, those preschool teachers may have no idea what to do with a child with special needs. They aren't normally trained for that and, meanwhile, the window for early intervention is closing.

I tell parents who are trying to decide whether or not they should get their child tested in any area that they should just do it. If they sense there's a problem, what harm does it do to check it out? If the test shows nothing is wrong, they can relax. But if there is a problem, they have not lost valuable time they needed to address it. Pretending it's not there doesn't mean it doesn't exist. And in the end, I think that parents should always trust their instincts about their children. They should not take no for an answer if they feel there's a problem, even if a professional tells them they're imagining things.

While Toby had been at CSHC, there had been several meetings about his transition from CSHC to the school district program. This culminated in a meeting with the head of the special needs department of our school district to decide whether Toby needed to be tested to see if he qualified for special education services at the district's preschool.

Once it was determined that the district would go ahead with the testing, the first step was to have the school psychologist come to our house to meet with us, do an interview, and run some tests with Toby. She was just wonderful. She immediately understood what we'd been through, and later we realized that her grandson was at the same school Toby would attend if he qualified.

She explained a little more about the program in our district. Apparently every district handles their special needs children differently. Some have a preschool program housed in a single location like ours. Some have small classes spread out at different buildings across their district. Some don't have a program, and send their special needs kids to a neighboring district. Some only offer limited private therapy. I am sure there are many other scenarios. I was grateful that ours was the way it was. I would go so far as to say that there are situations where it would be worthwhile for a parent to research different districts and consider moving to another one if their child needs help that is not offered where they live. It seems drastic, but the differences in services are vast and, depending on the issues, a move could be warranted.

Our district had consolidated all the preschool classes into one building. That way they had better access to specialists and could have an OT gym. Each class had up to twelve children with one teacher and one aide. Half of the children would have qualified for special needs services and would have an individualized education program (IEP). The other half would be typical peers. The typical students paid tuition just as they would at any private preschool. The children who qualified for services did not have to pay for school.

I had heard about this preschool before and it received rave reviews. Even so, I have to say that before I had Toby, I would never have considered sending my children there. I pictured it as a depressing place with rooms full of kids with medical equipment and other children banging their heads on the walls. I wondered what kind of behaviors typical children might pick up there.

That is a terrible stereotype, and it embarrasses me now that I was worried about it. I am admitting my bias here, though, because that's

---

individualized education program (IEP)

a detailed plan which is crafted for a specific child to help them reach age-appropriate educational goals

An IEP is an important tool for educators, therapists, and parents to document developmental status, establish realistic developmental goals for a child, and communicate the course of action for the next period of time. In the United States it must be regularly updated to reflect the current needs of the child and must be maintained as long as the child qualifies for special education.

---

what many people are picturing when they think of a special needs school. In reality, it was an educationally sound, sunny, happy preschool with highly trained professional teachers. In addition, the school administrators tried hard never to place more than one child with very significant needs in any one classroom so, in most classes, the majority of the special needs children just had a delay in some area such as speech or fine motor skills. Academically, it taught a lot more than the private preschool our girls had attended. I was impressed. This school actually had a year-long wait list for typical peer spots!

The children went to school four days a week with the younger kids attending in the morning and the pre-kindergarteners going in the afternoon. Specialists such as speech therapists, occupational therapists, and physical therapists came into the rooms on a rotating basis or pulled groups of kids out for special instruction. Otherwise, it looked like any typical preschool with various centers of blocks, books, and playdough.

The psychologist finished her interview with me and started Toby's assessment. She pulled out her black bag, and I immediately recognized it since everyone who had tested Toby had the same bag with the same testing materials in it. Toby remembered it too. The first assessment was a block test where the psychologist would show him a pattern and he was supposed to try and recreate it. The only problem was that Toby had memorized the test. When she set her bag on the table, Toby immediately reached in, pulled out her blocks and did the first pattern without her example. She laughed, and said, "Wow, he's great with patterns. You must be really good at math, Toby!" Then she modified most of her tests to try to get some kind of reading. I was laughing at the scene, but inside I still wondered if Toby's uncommon math skills had a deeper significance. I was also hoping that the psychologist realized that Toby had seen these tests several times. We really wanted to show that Toby needed services, and passing the tests with no effort was not going to help!

At the end of the meeting, she told us she had sufficient reason to bring him in for the full testing. She said his history alone would have made her recommend that course. Rather than sending multiple people out to test different areas, we were to come to the school on a testing day where they brought many kids in at once and all of the specialists took turns evaluating them. It was called a multifactored evaluation (MFE).

On the morning of Toby's MFE, I knew it would be a long day for him. He was just under three years old, and the MFE lasted several hours. I hoped he would make it through all the different areas. I shouldn't have worried. Toby was at his most motivated that day. He had always wanted to please his teachers, and today he tried harder than he ever had before. I thought he would be shy, and though he was a little hesitant, he wanted so badly to do well that he effectively had the best day of his life. Of course, it was on the one day I wished he would struggle a little!

He sailed through his speech testing with no trouble and even tested above average. There were a few articulation issues but nothing major. Not bad for a kid who only had a couple of sounds just one year before! Thanks, CSHC! This was no surprise, and it was wonderful, but again, we were really hoping he would qualify for services.

Next, Toby went with the adaptive physical education instructor and a physical therapist to evaluate his gross motor skills. I was sure he would test with at least a moderate delay in this area. He couldn't walk down stairs or step off curbs, and when he "ran" his feet never left the ground. He still couldn't jump without holding our hands. But Toby had the best day he had ever had. He chose that moment to jump for the very first time unassisted. He threw a ball. He ran, still without leaving the ground, but with the best form I'd ever seen. In fact, on his evaluation, the adaptive physical education teacher wrote, "Toby appeared to be learning skills during the evaluation!" Toby was so proud of himself and so was I, but I had a sinking feeling after the assessment when she said, "He's a little below average, but he's catching up quickly and seems to be doing fine!"

Toby's next stop was to play in a classroom with a child development specialist who would determine the level of his social and emotional behavior. He was fabulous! His behavior was well above his age level, testing in the four to five year range as a three-year-old. He was well behaved, courteous, good with other children and adults, taking turns and playing appropriately. As his mom, I was so proud, but couldn't he show any signs of difficulty?

The therapists and teachers started talking to me about his history. They couldn't believe it and they told me these results should not be possible. They looked at his intake reports from the county from one year prior and said they'd never seen anything like it. They called him "miracle boy."

The last person Toby had to see was the occupational therapist. I felt that this was our last chance, so imagine my dismay when the first thing she brought out was shaving cream. Of course. Toby had been working on touching shaving cream for the last six months in his therapy with Karen ever since she started the "car wash." It was about the only messy thing in the world Toby would touch. I couldn't believe the occupational therapist had chosen to test Toby with shaving cream on this day of all days!

Toby was still reluctant, eventually touching it briefly with one finger and then immediately asking to wash his hands. The therapist answered, "Oh, no, you don't need to wash your hands! We'll just wipe it off, no problem. When you get messy, you don't always need to wash your hands, right? You could wipe them on your shorts or a towel or whatever."

I was a little taken aback. I mean, why would a therapist encourage my son not to wash his hands? I was happy that he always wanted them clean. It was the only perk of SPD – I never had to worry much about germs. I asked her about it and she said, "A lot of kids with SPD end up developing OCD (Obsessive Compulsive Disorder) habits because of it. It's fine if he wants to wash his hands, and he should when he gets them dirty, but if he thinks he needs to wash them every time he touches something, that can get out of control quickly. We try to help children know they can wash their hands, but they aren't compelled to. They will still survive if their hands are messy." It was a new thought. I realized that they were seeing a lot of things I wasn't, and I was grateful for the tip.

She watched Toby play for a while, and asked me a lot of questions about his self-help skills like feeding and getting dressed. She also tried to get Toby to touch play sand and a few other surfaces and textures which he wouldn't do. Finally, she tested his fine motor skills for pre-writing development and, although he wasn't able to do everything she asked, he could do most of the exercises fairly well.

I knew that Toby's testing with her hadn't gone as well as the others, but considering that the fine motor assessment hadn't gone too badly and SPD wasn't a qualifying factor, I thought Toby had no chance of qualifying for services. They scheduled a meeting to go over the results the next day, and I went home and thought about ways to budget for private special needs preschool.

When we arrived the next day, all of the therapists and teachers who had done the testing were in a conference room along with several other people from the district. These meetings were always very formal and had some strict protocols that had to be observed. Everyone went around the circle and shared their findings about Toby. Over and over I heard how his skills were age appropriate, and in many areas above age appropriate. I also heard how much they enjoyed being with him and how hard he had tried to please them and do what they'd asked that day. He was called a delightful child with a sunny and friendly disposition. And there were many, many comments about his history and previous intake report and more people calling him "miracle boy." The speech therapist especially made a point of the fact that he had tested above average for speech, something that was almost unthinkable given the fact that he'd had so few sounds only twelve months earlier.

Finally, the occupational therapist gave her report. She spoke so quietly. She said that while many of Toby's fine motor skills were developing on target, his self-help skills were showing a "definite difference," the language used for a severe delay. Different areas of sensory processing were noted as a "probable difference" or "definite difference." She had observed Toby fall multiple times while moving to and around the classroom which indicated vestibular issues. His upper body lacked strength for everyday tasks. His limited hand strength made the pre-writing tasks difficult and was complicated by his SPD. His inability to feed or dress himself were severe self-help delays.

Then they said they were done and asked me to sign here. Sign what? What was I signing? The psychologist said, "You are signing that you understand that Toby has qualified for special education as a child with a disability. We need to have a second meeting to write his IEP, and then he can start school here in a couple of weeks."

I couldn't believe it. I hadn't even known self-help was an area that qualified a child for services! And because Toby had qualified, the teachers included all of his SPD therapies in his IEP. He was also going to get occupational therapy as part of school, although they suggested we continue our private therapy as well. The district occupational therapist would be working exclusively on school skills and we would need our private occupational therapist for food and strength issues. It was such an answer to prayer!

a note for parents

We know how fortunate we were to be in our school district. The more we talk to other parents, the more we realize how common it is to have to fight for help. Be persistent. Learn your rights. Do not give up because there *is* help out there although you cannot expect others to find it for you. You must be your child's advocate. You may be faced with questions and doubts, but keep going. It can be lonely, but you are not alone!

* Please see Appendix E for some helpful resources.

They told me they had discussed Toby's case at length, and everyone was so excited to see the progress he had made. He was absolutely a poster child for early intervention. They felt he would continue to make progress in the program, and that his history compelled them to offer that support. He was supposed to be three to start the program, but since his birthday was so close to the beginning of school, they let him start at the beginning of the year. This time, I went home and thanked God and tried to plan how to help Toby adjust to a whole new school.

CHAPTER 22

A New Season

Fall 2007 - Summer 2008

Th ere were many new beginnings in the fall of 2007. Toby started his new school, and Rachel began kindergarten at Rinnah's school. Since Toby's new school was close to his sisters' school, I estimated we were saving over ten hours a week in drive time alone. That was such a relief for all of us. I was finishing my second album and had my new radio promoter ready to release the songs. I was anxious to see where God would take our ministry.

Toby's transition to the district program went better than I expected. He was excited to try something new, which was an indication of how far he had come, and he remembered that the testing day at the school was a lot of fun. It helped that he still worked with the same private occupational therapist, Karen, and since she was at CSHC, he could visit his old teachers whenever he wanted.

Toby was assigned to Katie Rose's class, and he warmed up to her right away. The class had a similar structure to Toby's class at CSHC, but it was designed to eventually transition kids to kindergarten so it felt a little more "grown up." The class began with circle time, and then moved to centers which were areas with blocks or crafts or books or science that the kids could choose and explore. The large motor time was outside on the playground when the weather was nice or inside the gym when it was not. There was also a snack time in the cafeteria.

**Katie Rose, Toby, his friend, Hannah, and Toby's school
occupational therapist, Michelle McClellan**

Many of the centers were geared toward sensory experiences. Sometimes there was a center with play sand or water, or the craft would involve glue or glitter. Toby's favorite area by far was the block area. It was always clean, and he loved to build things. Katie would let him earn time in the block area by participating in areas he didn't like as well. His goals on his IEP included having him participate in messy crafts and touching and tasting foods he didn't prefer.

Again, I was struck by how "normal" this preschool was, and, at the same time, how incredibly well-trained the staff were. The children were having a great time, and learning so much. Much like CSHC, every single activity was planned with a purpose. What looked like a fun craft for Toby to make his parents a gift was also an occupational therapy device to get him to touch glue or learn to use scissors or strengthen his hand muscles and coordination.

The kids in Toby's new classroom had a variety of special needs. This was the district wide preschool so it did not specialize the way CSHC had. Some had qualified for speech or fine motor delays, one child had significant global delays, and one wore hearing aids. There were also many typical children, but, honestly, other than the severely delayed child in Toby's class, it was difficult to distinguish the special needs kids from their typical peers. Privacy issues meant the teachers couldn't discuss a child's diagnosis, and the parents generally didn't either. Over the years, I had several conversations with parents who were very surprised to learn that Toby wasn't a typical peer in the classroom.

I was extremely happy with the services we were receiving at the school, although I did miss a few things about CSHC. One huge difference for me was the lack of observation rooms. We were welcome in the class if we ever wanted to watch, but I knew that my presence was a distraction for Toby and it made separation more difficult for him so I only went a couple of times in his years there. This also meant it was harder to connect with other parents. We talked in the pick-up line, and there were a few opportunities for support groups, but we didn't have that daily interaction and I missed it. When I told Toby's new teacher, Katie, about the observation rooms at CSHC, she said, "Oh, that would be so wonderful. We wish we had that here, but we inherited this building, and there isn't money to retrofit for something like that. You were lucky to have a school with that luxury."

I realized then how very fortunate we had been at CSHC. Watching those classes through the observation window had taught me so much about what to do at home. I had no idea how uncommon observation rooms were. If I hadn't been able to watch that first year, it would have been so much harder to work on Toby's speech, food, and sensory issues in our daily lives. I think the fact that we worked on it all the time at home was a major factor in Toby's rapid gains, and I wish all families had the same access to learn about their child's therapy. Karen, Toby's private occupational therapist, told me that many parents expect to drop their kids off and have the therapist "fix" them, but it's just not realistic to expect a therapist to effect major gains in only one hour per week. I used to think of Toby's therapy as a training session for me because, as parents, we have our kids all day, every day. I now realize how much more parents and therapists can accomplish by working together.

A big difference for Toby at the new school was that the food portion of the day was really just a snack time. They did encourage Toby to eat different things, and part of his IEP was that he would "lick or taste one non-preferred snack item one time per week," but it wasn't the same well-crafted therapeutic tool snack time had been at CSHC. However, I understood that it wasn't necessary for most of the kids. This wasn't exclusively a speech classroom, and the majority of the children weren't dealing with food issues. Eating food was not necessary to complete school tasks. This was one area we would now need to tackle on our own.

Another change was the teacher to student ratio. Let's face it, we'd been completely spoiled by CSHC where the classroom had an unbelievable number of adults to very few children. I worried about how Katie would handle having so many students but I shouldn't have. She was amazing. Her assistant, Pam, was great too, and the class ran like clockwork. I thought there would be a lot more chaos with twelve preschoolers in one room, but anytime I dropped in, all the children were busily working away at their tasks, engaged and interested and happily learning. Preschoolers love predictability and order, and Katie did a great job of giving them a sense of ownership. They knew what was expected of them and what was happening next, and they loved it.

I also appreciated that this school followed the curriculum for the district, and as the kids got older, the program grew more academic. Toby was learning his letters and letter sounds, the months, weather and many other subjects. Rinnah and Rachel's private preschool hadn't covered many of the things Toby's class was learning, and I knew he would be more than prepared for kindergarten when he got there.

All in all, I realized that once again we had been blessed with a fabulous program for Toby. I wish I had known about the school during Rinnah and Rachel's preschool years; I would have sent them as typical peers.

Crafts as therapy

Toby started to feel at home there right away. He was unfailingly polite, and with his shy, big-dimpled smile, teachers were always trying to make him laugh. I was amazed that within days of starting school, anyone we would pass in the hall would call out to Toby, "Hey, little man, how's it going today?" or "Hey, Toby, where's that smile? I love that smile!" They all knew his name. He belonged there, and he knew it. It made his confidence soar.

Katie told me later that the occupational therapist who had qualified Toby came in to talk to her about him before he started. The therapist told Katie that Toby was one of the most severe sensory kids she had ever seen. He was actually fisting his hands and recoiling to avoid touching things, including the shaving cream that we had been working on for six months. She wanted to prepare Katie for the severity of Toby's SPD.

Later, Katie told me that Toby was the most severe case of SPD she had ever had in her classroom. I was really surprised by that, especially since we had made such tremendous progress before we even started the district program.

Since Toby's birthday is in the fall, he had three years at the preschool. In the first year, Toby continued to make tremendous progress. His improvement slowed down compared to his year at CSHC, and I could certainly see that early intervention window closing as he passed his third birthday, but it was still amazing to me. By the following summer, Toby was able to take a swimming class with me. He wasn't able to do it by himself yet, but with me, he was fine. He was able to play on any playground. His speech was well above his age level. He was choosing to play with playdough and in the sand box on purpose. He would help me cook and he wouldn't become upset if his hands got messy. He still liked to be neat, but he could handle it if he wasn't.

We even made some progress with food. Toby could eat chicken and rice and green beans now, and he would try a lick or bite of more things. We'd also discovered the joys of chocolate chip cookies, and if Toby knew there was a potential cookie at the end of a meal, he would try many more foods. His food choices were still severely limited, but his

By the end of this year Toby loved to play in the water and in the snow.

nutrition was no longer a concern. We were able to take him off of his supplements. One of the most satisfying moments in my parenting was throwing away that last bottle of supplements!

Another miracle occurred that year with Toby's hearing. We had to get a full assessment done again in the summer. Previously, we had been told that Toby's hearing was just barely in the normal range, and that he wasn't likely to make any more gains because of the scarring on his ear drums. He had been testing at about twenty-one before, and the doctors said the best we might hope for was eighteen. When we took Toby in that year, his numbers came in between six and eight, which put him in the completely normal range. They checked several times. There was no reason for it. His scarring had simply healed. Praise God!

That year also brought changes with my music ministry. I had a lot more invitations out of state, so I was traveling more, which made the kids' simplified driving schedules a real blessing for Nathan. Nathan's job offered some flexibility, and he could often manage to work from home when I was out of town. My mom was traveling with me more, or, if the schedule was too difficult at home, she would help Nathan with the kids and I would take another friend to help with my events.

My producer, Jon, and I worked on the new album all through the fall and I had the release concert for my second album, *Finding Beauty,* in December of 2007. Our new radio promoter, Wendell, decided to wait until after the Christmas season to begin the promotion, and the first single went out in January.

We did a limited release to selected stations that Wendell felt would connect with my sound. We also made the single available to the stations that had played my music from the first album. The response was decent considering I was a new voice to all of the stations Wendell was contacting. We started picking up more and more markets, and it opened new doors for ministry. I began visiting stations when I was traveling for concerts, and I did a lot of radio

A radio interview for *Finding Beauty*

interviews. Often it felt very surreal. Here I was, a mother of three from Ohio and a former classical voice professor sitting in on the morning shows, talking about the inspiration for my new songs and recording liners for the stations.

That spring I attended my first Gospel Music Association event in Nashville. It was held at the Renaissance Hotel downtown. I checked into my room on the twenty-third floor and headed back down for a mixer event. When I stepped into the elevator, I realized that the guy riding down with me was Jon Foreman, the lead singer of Switchfoot. I was so tongue-tied I didn't even say hello. Then I got off the elevator and literally ran into Mark Hall from Casting Crowns. When I recovered I realized that, yes, that was Bart Millard from Mercy Me getting coffee in the corner, and Mac Powell from Third Day was walking through the lobby trailed by a media team. This was certainly out of my comfort zone. What on earth was I doing here?

That event was so much fun. I will never forget it. I met a lot of people and did a few radio interviews with some of the stations who had delegates at the event. I finally met my radio promoter, Wendell, in person and was so grateful for his knowledge of the industry. I went to

At GMA with Mark Hall, Rebecca St. James, Bart Millard, Anita Renfroe, and Travis Cottrell

the teaching sessions and heard amazing music and soaked it all in. I was certainly a very minor player there, but that didn't change the fact that I was there. I just marveled at what God was doing.

That summer I also did my first television show with my music. I was asked to be on a show called *100 Huntley Street* which filmed in Toronto. It was a Christian talk show, and I didn't know much about it, but I was excited for the opportunity. I had been performing for so long that I rarely became nervous anymore, but I was going to have an interview and do two songs, and I was a little worried about it. It wasn't until we arrived at the hotel the night before that we learned the show was live and one of the longest running shows in Canada. It broadcasts to over thirty million homes and also goes worldwide. Now I wasn't just nervous, I was terrified! Nathan is always nervous for me even when I'm not, and when he saw me in that state, he was beside himself. I don't think I slept that night, and my call time was at seven in the morning. It went well, but it was God alone who got me through it. I've never been so happy to finish an hour in my life!

With all the changes in my career and at home, we were constantly challenged to keep our eyes on God. When I thought about the title of my new album, *Finding Beauty*, it was impossible not to realize that God was giving us beauty all around us. It had been two years since my dad's death and Toby's diagnosis. We had been through some of the darkest, hardest times of our lives. And here we were, beginning to catch glimpses of how God would use it for good (Romans 8:28). I couldn't wait to see what He would do next.

On *100 Huntley Street* to promote the new album

CHAPTER 23

An Ending and a Beginning

Fall 2008 - Summer 2009

W e started another year of therapy at the preschool and another year of ministry. That fall, I felt the Lord calling me to start speaking more. I had always shared about my dad, but now I was also sharing about Toby and our journey with SPD. People were always stopping me after concerts and church services to ask for more information to help children in their own lives. I also started speaking at women's retreats and events, teaching both from our personal experience and from the examples of people in the Bible. I was feeling very drawn to women's ministry.

We released a few more singles to radio, and my career was gaining momentum. My mom went with me on some longer tours where I would do concerts, speaking events, and guest worship at various churches. In between we would stop at radio stations all over the country promoting the new songs and sharing our story on the air. My mom had edited my dad's online journal of what God had taught him through his illness into a book called *Nobody Tells a Dying Guy to Shut Up,* and she was promoting that as well. It was exhausting, but it was also exhilarating. I was watching God open doors to places I had never even thought to go, and I could see Him using our story to bring people hope and encouragement. That year I went back to the Gospel Music Association event and sang a showcase for the industry people. I couldn't believe how much had changed in two short years.

Toward the end of that year, Toby's therapist, Karen, told us that he was doing so well that he no longer needed private occupational therapy. She did comprehensive testing on him again, and all of his scores were in the average and above average range. That was bittersweet. We were thrilled with his progress and the wonderful news! But Karen had been such a big part of our lives for those years. Toby loved her dearly and we were going to miss her. They had a party on their last day together, and this time Toby asked for cake!

One last leap into the ball pit!

Just after this, we had an amazing opportunity to go to the United Kingdom and then to Kenya on a music and missions tour. I had done the worship and a concert at a women's retreat in Michigan, and while there, I met a missionary from Kenya who was home on furlough. The next day, I led worship at a church a couple of hours away and her husband was there! It couldn't be a coincidence. After hearing my concert and my story, they asked us to come to Kenya for a month. I told them we couldn't leave our children that long, and they told us to bring them along. After praying about it, we accepted, and they started the process of organizing what would become a life-changing trip for us.

As we were planning the trip, we realized that our flight to Nairobi would connect through London, so I contacted a family friend who directs Young Life in the United Kingdom. We were able to go to England for a week to do some ministry with Young Life there. After that, we planned to spend the rest of the month in Kenya with African Inland Mission and World Vision in various cities, staying with different missionaries and doing concerts and ministry.

(Clockwise from left) Visiting an AIDS orphanage, giving a concert event at Rift Valley Academy in Kijabe, seeing World Vision in action near Malindi

Even though we were thrilled at the opportunity, I was concerned about how Toby would handle the trip. He was doing amazingly well now, but this was the same child who couldn't go outside two years earlier. Now we were taking him to Kenya. There would be no way to get his "safe" foods. The weather would be very hot, and the conditions very unpredictable. How would he handle it?

Our trip was also in May when school was still in session. How would this affect Toby's therapy and Rinnah and Rachel's class work? When I went to the schools to ask them how to handle the situation, I heard varying answers. One administrator told us to withdraw the kids from school for home schooling and then re-enroll them when we returned.

When I spoke to the staff at Toby's school about this idea, though, the principal said, "Oh, no. Don't do that! If you withdraw Toby, he will need to redo his testing when he returns. He's done so well here, there is no way that he will qualify for services now, and he would lose his place in his classroom. There's a long wait list for typical peers. I'll try to see if I can get the absences excused." In the end, we were able to get the absences excused for all the kids. In fact, the schools were wonderful, even supplying us with the work the kids would miss which we used to home school while we were away.

Getting licked by a giraffe

That trip stands out as one of the best family times we've ever had. Our kids were amazing, even on a thirty-four hour trip with three flights and a seven hour time difference. Toby rolled with the punches, just like his sisters. We tried to make sure he had his favorite kinds of clothes so he would be comfortable, and we looked for food options everywhere, but for the most part, Toby didn't need much special treatment. When we arrived in Kenya, we found a Nakumatt, the Kenyan equivalent of a supermarket, and spent way too much on a box of chocolate chip cookies to use as bribes so he would try new foods, but it was worth it. We were able to find chicken and rice most places which Toby was able to eat. Some of the missionaries had peanut butter toast, and that always made him happy. All of our kids loved the experience. Toby even fed a giraffe, which wrapped its long, slimy tongue around his hand to pull the food into its mouth. Toby thought it was gross, but hilarious, and he did it again and again. What a miracle for my son who couldn't stand to touch shaving cream as a toddler!

Dinner out with missionary friends in Kenya

That trip was inspiring in so many ways. We got to meet one of the African children that we have sponsored through World Vision for years, and it's hard to even put into words what it was like to be with him. We had prayed for this boy every day and kept his picture on our refrigerator for ten years and then there we were with him. We also visited camps for displaced peoples and brought clothing and did ministry at several AIDS orphanages and feeding centers for children living in desperate poverty. It opened all of our eyes and sparked in us a desire to get involved and share it with others.

When we returned, I found myself writing songs again, some of them inspired by our experiences in Africa. I spent the summer traveling back and forth to Nashville writing and recording my third album. My radio promoter was happy with the progress we had made with the singles off the second album, but he suggested that I work with someone who specialized in production for inspirational Christian music. I decided to do the album with Paul Marino, an acclaimed writer and producer with an extensive list of top national songs.

Nashville recording session for *Love Broke Through*

It was quite a leap of faith for us. The financial commitment was even greater, and I was out of my comfort zone again working with new people in a new place. We hired a publicist to coordinate an actual "release" this time. We had many big name session artists on the album, and the string players were all from the Nashville Symphony. At the recording sessions, I kept getting choked up. I couldn't believe I was there, and that these players were recording songs that I had written! My dad would have been so proud. And he would have said that he told me so.

How amazing to see what God had done in three short years. He had ordered our steps with Toby, transforming my terrified and shut down child into a confident, happy world traveler. He had led us through every step of the music ministry when we had no idea what to do next or how to pursue it. He had been faithful to us through all our grief over the loss of my dad and our struggles with Toby. God was definitely using it all to good. Now our story of God's faithfulness to my Dad and to me and throughout Toby's miraculous transformation were all woven together, and our ministry was just beginning.

CHAPTER 24

End of an Era

Fall 2009 – Summer 2010

T oby started his last year of preschool, and moved to the afternoon class along with the other older children. It was a kindergarten preparation class, and he loved it! One aspect that had been ideal for Toby was the preschool's policy that once a child was assigned to a teacher, the child kept that same teacher for his or her entire tenure. So Toby had Katie Rose as his teacher for three years, and I credit her with so much of his development. She had a wonderful way of pushing her students and not accepting anything less than their best effort while still letting them know that they were valued and loved and that she was proud of them.

That fall, Toby started playing soccer. Both Rinnah and Rachel played soccer for three seasons every year, so Toby had been going to games for as long as he could remember. The difference was that when he was little, it had been almost impossible to get him out of the car to watch a game without him panicking because it was windy and he had to walk on grass. If Toby did manage to watch a game, he did it sitting in a chair or with me holding him the whole time.

Now things were different. Toby was actually on the team. And he was good! We did have to look for shin guards that didn't irritate him texturally, but other than that, he had no problems. My child who had

Toby (far right) on the soccer field

screamed about changing his shoes and cried at the sight of grass was now wearing cleats, running through the field, and going for the ball. This same son who used to feel pain so intensely that he feared touch was getting knocked down in a group of boys and, instead of crying, was bouncing up laughing and trying again. It was truly a miracle.

Some things hadn't changed. Toby still loved math! He started asking me more questions about how to write two and three digit numbers. One day I told him to get me a piece of paper, and I had him write the numbers one through ten across the top. Then I wrote an eleven below the one and said, "See, this is the tens place and this is the ones place. So eleven is just ten plus one."

Toby said, "So twelve is ten plus two?"

"Yep."

"I got it. Thanks, Mom." Toby disappeared for a long time, and when he brought his paper back, he had taped more pages to the bottom and had written his numbers correctly all the way to 373. The only question he asked during the process was, "Is this called the hundreds place, then? Cool." During that year he also asked us to explain fractions and multiplication. I was still taken aback by Toby's incredible gift with math, but I was beginning to believe that maybe that was all it was. Perhaps it was simply a gift, not a symptom of any other disorder.

While all this was happening with Toby, we were also finishing up final details on the new album. We released my third album, *Love Broke Through,* that winter, and it really changed everything in our ministry. Suddenly I was on a lot of television shows and radio shows, and magazine articles were being written. It expanded our ministry tremendously, and I was so extremely grateful. We even had a top five national song, and two songs from the album made it onto the Billboard Top 40 radio chart. If you would have told me when Toby was born that I would have contemporary songs on the Billboard chart, I would have said you had lost your mind!

Television and radio appearances for *Love Broke Through*

I traveled a lot that year, doing radio tours, concert tours, and women's retreats and events. People frequently ask me what happens with my family when I am gone and how we handle that. The answer is that I have an incredible husband and family. Nathan is an amazing dad, and he does everything while I'm away. We've always been a team, and our kids know that they can come to either of us for anything. He is also my business manager and takes care of a lot of the details of the ministry. In addition, I'm blessed to have my mom travel with me often which helps tremendously, and sometimes she takes our children so Nathan can join me on shorter tours.

We began grouping events together into shorter time frames so I wouldn't have to be away from home more than a few days at a time. Another wonderful change that helped our family and ministry so much in that year was a new job for Nathan. He joined a different company, and was able to start working from home full time. This was an incredible blessing because Nathan was able to be home with the kids when I traveled. I work from home the rest of the time as well, so our kids have gotten used to having both of us around often. God has provided what we have needed every step of the way.

In May, we had to go in for Toby's annual IEP meeting. An IEP is rewritten with new goals every year, and Toby's old IEP was expiring. We had been warned ahead of time that they were going to discontinue it. He only had a month left of preschool, and it wasn't worth writing one for such a short period of time. No one thought he would need one in kindergarten.

**Backstage with Natalie Grant at a
women's event in Washington, D.C.**

We sat in the same conference room we had been in when the therapists had first told us that Toby qualified for services as a special needs child. We were in the same circle with almost the same group of specialists. As they went around giving their reports, all I heard was "above grade level," "at grade level," "advanced," and "goals were met." Even though Nathan and I knew how much progress Toby had made, it was almost hard to take in.

**Filming the music video for "God Loved
the World"**

I knew it was true. Toby was fine. He didn't need the support any more. I had peace about letting it go. But what a change from the meetings where we'd heard "definite difference," "severely delayed," "hearing impaired," and "medical issues."

It sounds as though I cry continuously, but I couldn't help but be emotional at that meeting. It was a happy conference, but it was also scary. These people had been our lifeline for many years at this point. I had at one time wondered if Toby would ever be able to function or communicate, but God had used this group of people to give me back my son. They had supported us and loved Toby and worked so patiently with him to get him where he was. Losing that support system, even when I knew it was time, was sad and a little frightening.

Since we were so close to the end, Toby was allowed to finish the school year. Nothing really changed for him except that he didn't meet with his school occupational therapist anymore. He still saw her in the classroom, and he just enjoyed his last couple of weeks. When we finished that year, he asked me several times if he would be allowed to come back to visit his teachers and I told him that he would. He was going to miss them, but he was really excited about kindergarten. He wanted to go to school with his sisters! He was going to be a big kid like them.

**Singing the national anthem for the
Pittsburgh Pirates**

That summer was a big one for all of us. I had some really fun and important shows including opening for Big Daddy Weave, and leading worship at an international conference in Washington D.C. We made a music video for one of my songs, "God Loved the World", and I was able to include all of our kids in it. They loved being a part of that, and we made it a visual representation of the Gospel. I also sang the national anthem at a Pittsburgh Pirates game and we all got to go and have a tour of the stadium from one of the owners.

Toby also started regular swimming lessons with his sisters, and it was just another reminder to me of how far we had come. When Toby was little, water felt like it was burning him. He could usually handle being in calm water such as a bathtub, but splashing was terrifying to him. All the visual chaos was overwhelming and the other children frightened him with their sudden movements. Now he was swimming, taking lessons with a group of kids who were splashing and flailing as they were learning, and he thought it was fun. I kept remembering when we would have to sit far away from the side of the pool while we watched his sisters. Now he was part of the action.

Fall was coming. Toby was set to enter kindergarten at the same school where Rinnah would be in sixth grade and Rachel would be in third. This time, Toby would go as a typical kid.

CHAPTER 25

A Typical Kid

Fall 2010 - Summer 2011

I was very nervous about Toby starting kindergarten. After all, he had been at the same school in the same room with the same teacher for three years. Now everything including his school was changing, and we had no support from an IEP. Would his new school listen to me? Would Toby be okay? Now he was going to be one of the youngest kids at a school full of older children, and he was supposed to go as a typical student! It seemed a lot to ask of our little guy.

Every time I had asked God for reassurance or peace in the last seven years, He had provided it. It wasn't always in the way I thought He would, but God had been faithful. I knew He hadn't changed, so we could trust Him with this too. God loved Toby, and God would lead us.

Fortunately, both of our girls attended Toby's new school, and I knew many of the teachers well. Toby was assigned to Ashley's class, the same class Rachel had been placed in for kindergarten, and it was a wonderful fit. I asked for a conference before the school year began, and sat down with Ashley to try to explain some of what Toby had been through. Katie Rose, his preschool teacher, also offered to talk with her and help with any issues. I wasn't extremely worried about Toby, but I wanted Ashley to know his history just in case. She was already familiar with sensory issues, and that made it so much easier.

**Toby with his kindergarten teacher,
Ashley**

As I was talking with Ashley, I realized that I had some mixed feelings about sharing Toby's story. I didn't want his teacher to have any preconceived ideas about him. He was doing so well, I didn't even know if it was important. But I also knew that there was a good chance that something would come up that would make more sense to her if she knew his history. Toby still reacted very strongly to pain. If he scraped his knee on the playground and seemed to overreact, I didn't want her to think he was just trying to get attention. If they had a class snack and he refused to eat it, I wanted her to know why. It was the idea of giving her helpful labels. In the end, I am glad I shared it with her since things did come up. I don't know what I will do when Toby begins first grade. We will have to decide year by year and teacher by teacher. Maybe one day, it won't even be necessary to talk about it.

Toby had a great first semester, and Nathan and I started to relax. He had a lot of friends, and I would go sometimes and have lunch at the school with all three of our kids. At Toby's table, it was fun to see the normalcy of the children all having fun together. Toby's acceptance of food continued to improve, and although he may always be somewhat picky, he can function at school and eat out and at other people's homes. It's totally workable.

In the winter we started having some new issues. Toby told me one day he was really homesick at school. I didn't think much of it but gave him an extra hug the next day. That afternoon, he came home telling me he was homesick again. Then I got an email from Ashley saying that he had gone to the nurse at lunch several days in a row saying that he was sick. We wondered if he was ill, but he didn't have any fever, and he seemed fine at home. I decided the long days of full-day kindergarten were catching up with him, and we should just do our best until Christmas break. Maybe he really was homesick. I visited him more at lunchtime and he was clingy and sad, and not acting like himself at all.

After Christmas break, I thought the problem would improve since Toby had spent so much time at home with us, but it didn't. If anything, it got worse. He was crying a lot, and it always seemed to center around lunch time. I started asking a lot of questions. "Is someone being mean to you? Are the kids fighting during lunch recess? Is something making you sad?" It sounded to me like he was being bullied. He kept telling me no. No one was being mean, he liked everyone, no one was having a problem. He was just so homesick and he wanted to stay home with me!

This went on for weeks. It got to the point that Toby was near tears most of the day. He was so worried about being homesick at lunch that it affected his entire day, and he didn't want to go to school. I didn't know what else to do. It seemed to match so well with bullying that I went to watch him at lunch and recess. I noticed that it was very icy, and there was a lot of visual chaos on the playground with many kids running around. Toby was always more nervous on icy surfaces. But when I asked if he'd rather stay inside for recess, he looked horrified and said, "No! How would I play with my friends? I love recess!"

One day, I went to see Toby at lunch again, and he begged me to stay with him at recess. I was feeling like an enabler, but I couldn't leave him crying in the hall, so we went outside. Maybe I could figure out what was going on! Toby was doing okay, so I told him I was going home and he started to cry. All of a sudden, three little boys ran up to him: his cousin, Owen, and his friends, Adam and Sam. They all started asking Toby to play, and finally, Sam said, "Toby, we're going to do whatever you want today because we're your best friends! We're going to make you happy again! What do you want to do, because we're going to do it!" What sweet boys! I realized Toby had a lot of friends who really liked him. There wasn't anything bad happening on this playground. It had to be something else, but what?

I remembered that Toby had struggled last winter as well in the preschool. He had gotten very teary and couldn't control his emotions. We suspected he wasn't sleeping well because his iron was low again after taking him off supplements. Our daughter, Rinnah, had been anemic when she was younger and had experienced sleeping issues when her iron levels were low. When we started Toby's iron supplement again, he improved almost immediately.

This time was different, though. We couldn't find a medical reason. I called the pediatrician and had a long talk with the nurse who told me she could recommend some pediatric psychologists. She said that Toby was probably having emotional problems and that we should look at medicating him. I tried to explain that this was new behavior and I didn't think a child would develop emotional problems in a matter of weeks. She didn't have any other solutions, though, and offered again to connect us with counseling or medication. It didn't make sense to me, and I knew we weren't going to medicate Toby without more proof that there was a need.

Finally, I spoke to my friend, Jenny, about my concerns. I was really worried. Kindergarten had been going so well and it was very discouraging to have Toby make the transition beautifully just to lose it all in the middle of winter. What was going on?

Jenny's son has sensory issues too. She said, "I really think you need to look at the sensory angle here. This sounds like a problem of overload to me. He's probably not even aware of it. It's always at lunch, right? And you know it's not bullying. What's happening at lunch that would be bothering his sensory system?"

I started adding things up. It was hot in the building and very cold outside. The playground had been icy for weeks which made balance more difficult. Lunch recess was the only time when all the kids from all the grades were together on the playground, so it was the most visually chaotic and noisy time of the day, and it was also intimidating as a kindergartener to have all those big kids running around while standing on ice. Finally, I remembered that the teachers had all the kindergarteners put on their coats before lunch because the children have trouble with their zippers. They would eat in their bulky winter coats, getting very warm, and then go outside into the cold. So we had temperature, balance, clothing, visual, and sound overload.

My doctor once gave me an example of the triggers for migraines. He said, "It's like all the little things add points and when you reach one hundred, wham, you get a migraine. So, maybe your morning coffee was thirty-five points, your stress level is another thirty, and your lack of sleep is twenty. You're also dehydrated which is another ten points, but you're still doing fine, sitting there with ninety-five points. Then you walk out of my office and the sun hits you in the eyes, and normally that would be nothing, a little five-pointer, but it was all you needed to send you over the edge, and suddenly you have a migraine."

A similar theory works to explain sensory overload, and in this case, there were just too many factors at once. Toby could deal with his bulky coat or the change in temperature from inside to outside or the kids on the playground. All of these things were doable, but not when they were all simultaneous. It was a perfect storm of sensory issues right at lunchtime. And Toby was just a kindergartener. He didn't know why he couldn't handle it, he just knew it was too much and he couldn't take it. Then he became sad and wanted his mom. In his mind, he must be homesick!

I talked with his teacher, Ashley, about my theory, and we discussed ways we could take the edge off of the sensory overload at lunchtime. My proposal was that she allow Toby to go to lunch without putting on his coat first. Then he could stop back at the room and grab his coat before he went outside which would keep him from such extreme temperature changes. Ashley was happy to try it.

That was all it took. Within two days he was able to make it through lunch without tears. Within a week he was beginning to believe he might like school again. Within a month, he'd totally forgotten it had ever happened. The weather started to change and it got easier and easier. I went to school occasionally to have lunch with the kids, and now Toby yelled, "Bye Mom! See you later!" and ran out onto the playground with his friends. It was exactly the way it should be.

I feel the need to say here that I know there are many, many schools out there which never would have said, "Sure, fine, let's try that!" about the coat. There are many places that would have required an IEP for the coat, and if a child didn't have a formal plan, nothing would have changed. I've talked to so many parents who have had a terrible time getting appropriate help from their school districts.

Recently, I spoke with a mother whose son has a diagnosis of Asperger's Syndrome (a form of autism) which in any district in the country should have resulted in an automatic IEP. She had to fight her district for two years, eventually writing the superintendent and threatening to sue the school district before she received one. Her son's teacher told him that he was just "a bad boy" and had ADHD. The teacher wanted him to be medicated, and she even knew which medications she wanted him to take.

So I feel doubly fortunate to have had a teacher who was so willing to work with us and to live in a school district that has been so supportive. The change we asked for was minor. It meant that Toby was allowed to go back into his classroom for an extra minute every day to get his coat. But that small change enabled Toby to function and even enjoy school. His teacher didn't have to spend so much time trying to calm him down, and ultimately it was a benefit not just to him, but to his entire class.

I don't know what will happen next year. Looking back, I'm sure that some of Toby's problems in the winter in preschool were due to his iron being low, but I'm also sure that more of it was due to sensory stress when the weather was so cold. We probably just started him on iron when the weather was changing and assumed that fixed everything. You can bet that next winter, if Toby starts acting sad, we will be looking at sensory solutions first. I am so glad we didn't medicate him for a problem he did not have.

After that change, Toby went back to enjoying kindergarten. He loved every minute of it. He loved playing with all the kids, he loved learning, he loved art and music and gym. He loved it all! His next report card was literally perfect. There were no areas in which he could have scored higher. We were so proud of him, and just amazed at how things had changed.

We realized that it was time to move on a bit. We were no longer using the bounce house where Toby had learned to jump. Toby hadn't needed it for years. I considered selling it in a garage sale, but then thought to ask Toby's preschool teacher, Katie, if she had anyone in her class who could use it for therapy. She wrote back and asked if the preschool could possibly have it. They would use it in their OT gym. I asked Toby what he thought of that. He was feeling a little sentimental about getting rid of something he had enjoyed so much, but then he said, "That's perfect! Then it can help lots of boys and girls." We took it over after school one day, and his former occupational therapist hugged him and thanked us for all the kids who would use it.

One day, Toby's kindergarten class had an open house. The parents could come and see what the kids had been working on in all the different learning centers in their classroom. Toby was leading me from center to center, showing me his writing and reading to me in the book corner, telling me where we lived on the map and what the weather was like today. Then he took me to the math center. All of the kids were

One last jump to say goodbye to the bounce house

rolling a pair of dice and there was a big bowl of plastic spiders in the middle of the table. If a child rolled a three and a one, he would get three spiders and one spider and then count them together and write on his worksheet, "3+1=4."

Toby picked up the dice and then pulled my head down to whisper in my ear. "Mom, sorry, I forgot, I have special dice. Wait here." He ran over to his mailbox and grabbed a container of dice. These dice went from thirteen to nineteen. Then he whispered to me again, "I'm not really supposed to talk about it. I don't want to make anyone feel sad."

He stood at the table with three other children and rolled his dice. He got a nineteen and a seventeen. He sighed. Slowly he started counting out nineteen spiders from the bowl. His teacher walked by and saw him and stooped down to whisper in his ear, "Remember, bud, it's fine with me if you want to just do them in your head. It takes a long time to get that many spiders!"

He brightened immediately and grinned at her. "Okay!" Without a second thought, he wrote, "36" and kept moving. He finished his sheet before the girl next to him had done her third problem. Her mom said to me, "Wow, that's incredible!" Looking at Toby, she asked, "Where did you learn all that math?"

Instantly, I thought back to the first time I had realized that Toby was exceptional with math. I remembered all my fears about it indicating something abnormal, and our years of worry about what Toby's future would hold. I thought about when he couldn't touch anything or eat or communicate. How he had cried anytime we left him with other children or adults. And I remembered God's faithfulness to us and the years of therapy and help and all the progress Toby had made. I thought of all of God's promises to us during the tragedies we'd been through and the celebrations as well. I remembered that just that week Toby had been talking about our upcoming summer vacation to the beach and how he was planning to bring his boogie board to play in the waves with his dad. And I wondered how many miraculous ways God would use Toby's story in the future that we hadn't even imagined yet.

So many thoughts were stirred up by that simple question. Everything had changed. Toby's math skills were a gift from God. They weren't some sinister symptom of a disorder; they were a blessing that the Lord had given. Nathan had been right all those years ago.

And so I answered her, "Oh, Toby loves numbers. He's just good at math!"

Rachel, Rinnah, and Toby at the beach

Appendixes

Appendix A[*]

Sensory Processing Overview

1. What is Sensory Processing?†

Sensory processing is a term that refers to how a person's brain interprets and responds to sensory input from their own body and the world around them.

Most people are familiar with the five senses, but in actuality there are seven:

1. Touch (tactile)
2. Proprioception (awareness of body position and input to muscles and joints)
3. Vestibular (awareness of head position and movement; important for balance)
4. Sight
5. Sound
6. Taste
7. Smell

Efficient sensory processing is an important part of everything we do in our daily lives. We rely on accurate information from our senses to

---

* Content in Appendix A used by permission of the **Columbus Speech & Hearing Center** - http://www.columbusspeech.org - (614) 263-5151
© 2011 Columbus Speech & Hearing Center

† http://www.columbusspeech.org/speech-and-occupational-therapy/occupational/sensory-processing

learn new things, to do our daily activities at school, work and home, and to know whether or not we are in danger. Sensory processing is a foundation for all of our other skills.

Sensory Integration/Sensory Processing

Pat Fasick, OTR/L

Sensory processing can be characterized as the "foundation" of a house. If your foundation is not stable, you may have structural problems in the other areas of your house. Therefore, problems with sensory processing can cause difficulties in other areas of functioning, such as behavior, learning, motor skills, play and social skills, attention and speech-language development.

2. What is Sensory Processing Disorder?‡

A sensory processing disorder occurs when a person's brain or nervous system does not respond accurately or efficiently to sensory input. In the most simple terms, this may be due to an over-response to a

‡   http://www.columbusspeech.org/speech-and-occupational-therapy/occupational/spd

sensation, or an under-response to a sensation. This can lead to a variety of problems, including behavior and emotional issues, difficulty with learning, and delayed development of age appropriate skills.

Sensory processing disorders are also sometimes referred to as Sensory Integration Dysfunction. This term was first coined by Dr. A. Jean Ayres, a prominent occupational therapist and neurobiologist who conducted extensive research on the topic. All individuals are unique, and have different tolerances and thresholds for sensory input. For example, some people are very ticklish while others are not; some people like to work with background music on, while others prefer silence to focus. It is when an individual's sensory responses to sensory input are so extreme that it interferes with their day-to-day life that there is a problem.

3. What are the signs of Sensory Processing Disorder?[*]

Sensory processing disorders may look different in each individual due to which sensory systems are affected, the severity, and the person's own unique nature. However, some general characteristics may include any one or more of the following:

Touch (Tactile) Sensory Processing:

- Avoids or becomes upset with unexpected touch input; pulls away from hugs and kisses
- Extreme overreaction to having hair washed or cut, nails trimmed, getting dressed, changing diaper, etc.
- Overly sensitive to certain textures. For example, doesn't like to get hands messy with playdough, finger paint, or sand
- Avoids or becomes upset about wearing certain clothing; for instance, only likes sweatpants and won't wear jeans, or needs to have socks turned inside-out
- Seems to be unaware of touch; is unaware of messiness on face or hands

---

[*]   http://www.columbusspeech.org/speech-and-occupational-therapy/occupational/spd-signs

- Shows little reaction to scrapes or bruises (unusually high pain tolerance)
- Is unaware what he/she is touching unless looking at it

Proprioception and Vestibular Processing:

- Uses too much or inappropriate force or pressure when playing with others or with toys
- Seems to have poor balance; trips or falls often
- Has poor body awareness; bumps into people or objects frequently
- Dislikes playground activities, such as swinging, sliding, or climbing
- Uncomfortable on elevators or escalators; anxious about heights or falling, even when no real danger exists
- Seek movement constantly; has trouble sitting still or staying in a seat
- Seeks spinning, twirling, and swinging for long periods of time; may appear to not get dizzy
- Seems to have a loose and "floppy" body; seems weaker and tires more easily than other children
- Tends to slump or lie down rather than sit upright; constantly props head with arm or hand, or puts head down on desk

Motor Planning and Coordination:

- Appears "clumsy" and has trouble learning new motor tasks; seems to have "two left feet"
- Difficulty using tools such as eating utensils, writing tools, scissors, combs, etc.
- Difficulty using feet and hands together, like to throw or catch a ball or to do jumping jacks
- Doesn't have a hand preference after age four or five; switches hands frequently during writing or drawing tasks; doesn't seem to use either hand well

Auditory Processing:

- Has trouble discriminating between similar words and sounds even though you know his/her hearing is okay
- Trouble with following directions
- Trouble making conversation
- May become overly upset with loud or sudden noises
- Has trouble paying attention when there is background noise
- Is distracted by noises that go unnoticed by others; for example, a car driving by outside
- Is delayed with speech and language development

Visual and spatial processing:

- Has trouble with puzzles, shape sorters, or other activities requiring recognition of shapes and patterns
- Lags behind peers with learning to recognize and write letters and numbers; confusion of letters like b, p, and d, g and q, etc.
- Has trouble shifting gaze from one object to another, such as from a blackboard to his/her own paper; loses place easily when reading
- Has a poor sense of direction; confuses right/left, up/down, before/after, etc.

Oral Sensory:

- Unusually picky eater; limits self to certain tastes, textures, or temperatures
- Seems unaware of food in mouth; overstuffs mouth or spills food from mouth
- Gags or refuses to try new foods
- Messy eater; gets food all over hands and face and doesn't seem to notice or care
- Gets upset if hands or face get messy with food; won't even touch certain foods

Smell:

- Overly sensitive to smells; bothered by smells that go unnoticed by others
- Seems unaware of smells

Learning and Behavior:

- Has trouble sequencing, organizing, and carrying out the steps of a task
- Trouble with problem-solving and figuring out something new
- Easily frustrated
- Reluctant to try new things
- Low self-esteem
- Difficulty making friends and relating to peers

If you have any concerns about your child's sensory processing, he or she may benefit from an occupational therapy evaluation.

DO YOU KNOW ME?

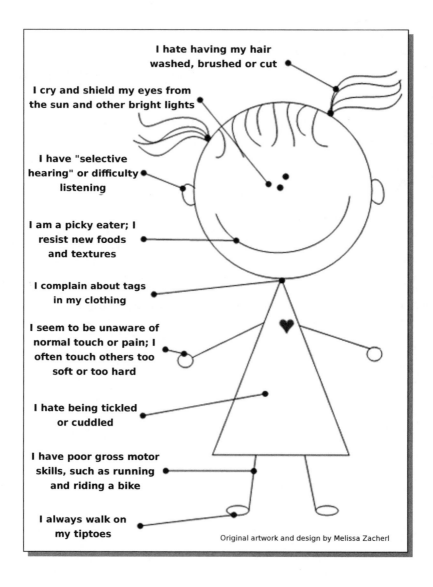

I hate having my hair washed, brushed or cut

I cry and shield my eyes from the sun and other bright lights

I have "selective hearing" or difficulty listening

I am a picky eater; I resist new foods and textures

I complain about tags in my clothing

I seem to be unaware of normal touch or pain; I often touch others too soft or too hard

I hate being tickled or cuddled

I have poor gross motor skills, such as running and riding a bike

I always walk on my tiptoes

Original artwork and design by Melissa Zacherl

Do You Know Me?

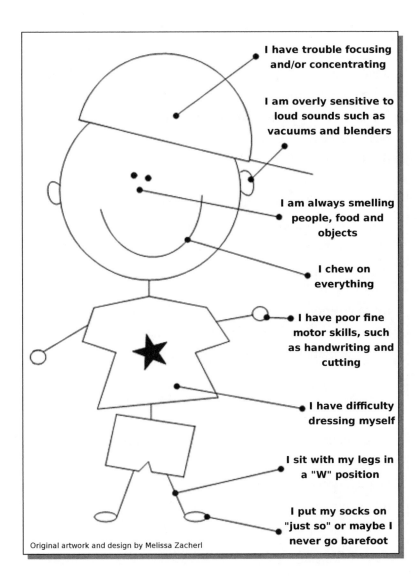

I have trouble focusing and/or concentrating

I am overly sensitive to loud sounds such as vacuums and blenders

I am always smelling people, food and objects

I chew on everything

I have poor fine motor skills, such as handwriting and cutting

I have difficulty dressing myself

I sit with my legs in a "W" position

I put my socks on "just so" or maybe I never go barefoot

Original artwork and design by Melissa Zacherl

I'm a Sensational Kid!

I mean, I have **Sensory Processing Disorder**. That just means that my brain can't process sensory information the right way. When my brain gets information through any of my senses – sight, smell, hearing, taste, touch, vestibular, or proprioception – it doesn't always know what to do with that information and I become very disorganized and confused. Sometimes I overreact to this sensory input and sometimes I don't react enough. This makes it *really* hard for me to function at school, in public and even at home. I might have trouble learning or making friends. I might be really shy and withdraw from everyone, even my own mom! I might have trouble coping and have a lot of tantrums and meltdowns. I might be afraid of a lot of activities that kids usually enjoy. It's super tough.

So, *Do You Know Me?* Or maybe someone like me? Well, there are lots of things you can do to help me. Being patient and understanding is a great place to start! But then you need to talk to my doctor or an Occupational Therapist and they can help you to help me feel better, learn better, behave better, and *get better!*

Oh, yeah! I really *am* sensational, by the way!

A Conversation with Speech and Language Pathologist, Stacey J. Gall, MA, CCC, SLP/L

JENNIFER: I'm here with Stacey Gall who is a speech language pathologist and the coordinator of the preschool program at the Columbus Speech and Hearing Center.

Hi, Stacey.

STACEY: Hi, Jennifer. Good to see you.

JENNIFER: Good to see you too. So tell us a little bit about your program here.

STACEY: Well, the program that Toby participated in was the Toddler Language Class (TLC), one of the Columbus Speech and Hearing Center's classroom-based early intervention programs. TLC was developed to serve very young children with speech and language delays. It's designed to look and function like a typical, high quality toddler preschool, with one main exception. It's taught by an early intervention specialist and a speech language pathologist, and an occupational therapist joins the class one day each week. This team of professionals adapts all the naturally occurring classroom activities to meet each of the children's developmental needs. The curriculum is play-based and set within a predictable daily routine.

JENNIFER: And who do you serve in the Toddler Language Class?

STACEY: Children as young as 18 months to 3 years of age who have been diagnosed with a primary deficit in expressive language with no other, as of yet identified, developmental areas of concern. Children are referred by the Franklin County Board of Developmental Disabilities (FCBDD), Help Me Grow, speech language pathologists, and friends or families who have previously enrolled children in the program.*

JENNIFER: You say they are delayed in expressive language. Can you explain the difference between "receptive" and "expressive" language?

STACEY: Receptive language refers to the ability to *understand* what others are saying. Expressive language refers to the ability to *say* things to others.

It's normal for young children to understand much more language than they are able to use. This is the natural progression of language development. But with a child who has age-appropriate receptive language and delayed expressive language skills, the difference is disproportionate. These children are trying to communicate any way they can: looking at you intently while pointing, gesturing, pantomiming, grunting, and vocalizing, but few comprehensible words are produced.

JENNIFER: You are a speech and language pathologist. What is the difference between "language" and "speech"?

STACEY: Expressive language is the way we use words to communicate to others, such as talking, writing, and sign language. Speech is the act of using the mouth to articulate sounds, and sequence sounds into words and phrases. So, language has more to do with thinking and knowing, while speech is essentially a motor activity.

An occupational therapist once told me, "Speech is the finest of fine motor actions." If you think about all the muscles and body systems that

---

Both FCBDD and Help Me Grow are names of programs in the state of Ohio. Local names for these programs will vary.

need to coordinate for speech, it is amazing! You need to coordinate your lips, jaw, tongue, voice, breath support and more, all at the same time and within milliseconds.

JENNIFER: And how does an occupational therapist fit into a speech classroom?

STACEY: Over the years, we've noticed that many of the children who demonstrate a moderate to severe expressive language deficit accompanied by age-appropriate receptive language skills have subtle fine motor issues and/or sensory processing issues, but not necessarily to the degree that would be identifiable as a disorder. Since speech is a fine motor activity, and since sensory processing is the foundation for all learning and development, it's important to have an occupational therapist, the professional who specializes in these areas, participate in the program.

JENNIFER: And what is the role of sensory development? I was very surprised, when we started, to hear you say that the incidence of sensory disorders was so high in relation to speech delay. How do you approach sensory issues in your program?

STACEY: The ability to process or "make sense" of what you are hearing, seeing, touching, smelling, tasting, of how you are moving and balancing your body, is the foundation for everything we do. When someone has trouble processing this basic information there is a weak foundation for learning. So, if a child has trouble processing auditory, visual, or movement information, he may be challenged to make sense of the speech sounds he *hears* you say, the way your mouth moves when he *sees* you say it, or how to *move* his mouth to make the same sounds.

So we provide an environment where children have the opportunity to participate in a variety of carefully chosen sensory experiences. Some children can be described as "sensory seekers" and others as "sensory avoiders." If the degree of seeking or avoiding impacts a child's ability to participate in typical activities with his peers, that's a problem. The goal, then, is for the "avoiders" to be able to take baby steps to increase their tolerance and participate in activities with confidence, and for the "seekers" to be able to decrease the intensity of their participation so that their peers are able to join them.

JENNIFER: As a speech pathologist why do you think that speech delay can be one of the first signs of sensory processing disorder?

STACEY: I think it's because talking is a milestone that's on parents' radar, and is easily observed. When did she say her first word? How many words does my child have by eighteen months, twenty-four months, and so on. Symptoms of SPD can be more subtle, attributed to personality, and easily explained away or overlooked at this young age.

It's common to hear, "He's a boy, he'll grow out of it," "His father was just like that," or "He's had a lot of ear infections, let's allow those to resolve." Those things may be true, but wouldn't you rather have an assessment to either rule out or identify a problem *now*, rather than wait another six months or a year to find that there is a problem and think, "Oh my gosh, I've just lost six months or a year."

JENNIFER: And of course with the window of opportunity for early intervention being up to age three, those six months can be really significant.

STACEY: They can be. And that's the reason there is a TLC program. It's understood, now, how much brain development happens in those first three years. While a brain continues to make new connections after age three, it also goes through a period called pruning, like pruning a tree, where circuits that are not used get removed. The best time for learning some of these foundation skills is before three years of age, and we have seen that over and over.

It's kind of funny, at the end of the year some families will say, "Yeah, we really loved your program, but my child probably would have caught up anyway." And that could happen, but the interesting thing is that in the eighteen years that I have been doing this with sixteen kids a year, it's amazing how many of the TLC kids really do catch up. And we don't see the same rate of progress in the kids who enroll in our preschool program a year older who didn't have prior access to early intervention.

JENNIFER: This is such an important point to me. Because Toby was twenty or twenty-one months old and the advice I was given was, "Let's give it six months or a year." If we had waited that long to start the testing process, we would have missed that window. Now I know that he still would have improved after age three, but I don't think we would have seen such a dramatic difference.

STACEY: It's not so much a window of opportunity slamming shut, although it's often overgeneralized that way. But this is a period of development where you can have *more* efficient, *more* effective developmental progress and impact.

JENNIFER: That was certainly key for us. Can you talk about some of the techniques you use here to help kids with their expressive language?

STACEY: Sure. The three main goals of TLC are to improve awareness, strength and coordination of the mouth and other structures for speech; to increase the "inventory" of speech sounds for saying words; and to increase the number of words and word combinations to communicate with others.

One example of a method we use in class is brushing the kids' teeth. When we brush kids' mouths, we are helping them with their *body* awareness. If you close your eyes you can touch your nose without seeing it, because you know where your body is in space, where your nose is relative to your hand. For example, when children don't have that body awareness in relation to their mouth, they can't plan where to put their tongue to make a "t" sound, or how far to open their jaw for an "ah" sound. So when we brush their teeth we are also naming the places and spaces in the mouth to help them develop a mental image, a map, so when we talk about our tongue tip, or talk about putting our lips together, they can think about how it feels and what it would look like, without being in front of a mirror.

Most of the techniques we use are incorporated into the kid's play. For example, to encourage a child to start to imitate the "b" sound we'd find ways to make that the sound effect for something. Perhaps we are playing with a boat, and we are using the sound, "buh, buh, buh, buh, buh" because that's the sound this boat makes. We are giving him a *reason* to try and make this new sound or do this new movement with his mouth.

JENNIFER: Yes, and you know, the kids love school. Toby never thought, "Oh, I'm going to therapy." Toby thought, "This is the most fun I've ever had!"

STACEY: When someone's watching us in our preschool program they may be thinking, "Wow, all they're doing is playing in there! What are the teachers doing and where is the therapy?"

Young children learn through play. Adults think about learning as receiving information and then understanding it and using that information. But that's not the way children learn, especially at age two. Kids are still learning cause and effect; that water flows in one direction and a ball rolls down an incline. Kids learn everything through play and everyday experiences. So, just telling a young child something doesn't teach him a thing.

Imagine that you are trying to help a child say, "apple." Adults might say, "Say apple. Say apple! Here's your apple. Use your words. Say apple! I'm sorry you can't have the apple, you didn't try to say apple." That does nothing to teach a child how to communicate. But if a child looks at the apple and goes, "uh," and I know that the child wants an apple, that's a perfect learning opportunity for me to say, "Apple? You want an apple! I love apples. Let's eat an apple. Here, I'm going to cut it up. Ah, ah, ah, ah, apple, ah, ah, ah, ah, apple." I'm giving lots of models of the word or maybe just exaggerating one of the sounds in the word. Now, because it's something that the kid is totally interested in, I have his *full* attention.

He's watching the way my mouth moves when I say the word. We do that all day long in our interactions with the kids.

When children come to our class, one of the first things we want them to know is that we as teachers recognize that they are competent communicators, and that we will understand many of the things that they are trying to tell us. We respond to *what* a child is telling us, not *how* he is saying it. So by reducing the frustration associated with talking, the children become more relaxed, willing to take risks and try new challenges.

JENNIFER: That reminds me of when Toby started TLC here. His frustration was so alleviated as he realized he was being understood and that he could communicate.

STACEY: Right! We're not going to try to get a child to say something that he can't yet say. Reducing the frustration associated with communication will reduce anxiety. The children can then feel like, "I'm ready to learn and here's some fun stuff," and they will just jump in. It's all play and it *has* to be play to be effective learning for two-year-olds.

JENNIFER: Please tell us about the OT gym, which was Toby's favorite thing in the program.

STACEY: The OT gym is this fantastic space where children have the opportunity to climb, jump, swing, roll, crash, and bounce in a safe environment. There are all kinds of mats and giant foamy pillows. There is a big ball pit, a jump island, and a climbing wall. There are many different kinds of swings that we can hang from the ceiling.

All of this helps to activate and coordinate the sensory processing in the body. Feeling the impact of jumping on the joints and the muscles, feeling the impact of using your arms when you are climbing or hanging on a trapeze, or experiencing the impact of swinging and gravity, whether it's in a line or in a circle, all helps to pull the brain together. Also, movement really facilitates making sounds. If you're on a giant ball you are going to go, "whoa, wow, woo, wee" and practice a bunch of different sounds. Of course, the kids don't know they are practicing. They are just imitating me making goofy sounds while they roll around on a ball.

JENNIFER: Talk a little bit about the role of food in your classroom. Food was a major challenge for us for years, and a difference that I noticed when we switched to the school district program was that food was a big part of the therapy every day here and it wasn't as much elsewhere. Why do you use food and how do you use food?

STACEY: You can play with food in ways that can help improve the awareness and coordination of the mouth. We can pretend to hold a pretzel sideways between our lips like a dog holding a bone. Or we can rub the bumpy, salty pretzel on our lips and tongue. It's kind of a continuation of that teeth brushing idea. And of course, it has a role in sensory development.

Many of the kids who enroll in our class have food aversions or a limited number of foods that they will eat. Our approach to food and snack-time helps some children reduce their food anxiety and become motivated to try new things. The first thing the children need to know is that they don't have to eat any of it. "You don't like that? Well, don't eat it. It just needs to stay on your plate."

This is how Toby went from running away from the table if there was a dab of pudding on his plate, to being able to tolerate pudding on his plate, to being able to pick up a "safe" food like a pretzel stick and touching or stirring the pudding on his plate. Now he is interacting with the food, where before it was, "I see pudding! My gut response is fight-or-flight. I'm out of here."

JENNIFER: At home, Toby couldn't sit at the table, let alone have something on his plate when we started. He had a hard time even being in the room.

STACEY: It's really a combination of earning a child's trust and taking baby steps. Once Toby understood that we were not going to *make* him eat something, or *tell* him to eat it, or *trick* him into eating it, he was able to stay at the table. We start wherever the kids are.

If a child can't tolerate a food on his plate, then it goes on a napkin next to the plate. If the napkin is not going to work, we put it on another plate in the middle of the table, not even within his reach. "That's yours, you don't have to eat it, but that's yours, it just has to be there." If that's all he needs to be able to hold it together and stay at the table and be with his friends, that's what we'll do. Then, gradually, over time, we can move the "dreaded food" closer, until he can tolerate interacting with it. Once a child is able to interact with a food, stirring it, plopping raisins on it, covering it with crackers, he is getting closer to actually tasting it.

JENNIFER: And isn't food aversion just a huge thing with parents?

STACEY: Yes, it is. Because the parent is thinking, "I want my kid to be healthy. He needs to eat vegetables to be healthy." So you start trying to chop up vegetables really small, and sneak them into a favorite food. But when your child finds it, you're busted! The child thinks, "Mommy knows I don't like this. She tried to hide it. I can't trust that favorite food anymore." Then the child loses another food from an already limited food repertoire. You just can't break that trust.

JENNIFER: I will point out to people that Toby is now in kindergarten and he eats better than most children I know. So obviously it does work over time. We truly believe Toby would not be eating now without our involvement at home in addition to school; he needed that support with every food encounter that he had for all those years.

STACEY: That's a very important point. Some children, like Toby, need that support with every food. You can't just wait it out and expect that when they're hungry enough they'll eat.

JENNIFER: Speaking of parental support, how would you rate the importance of parental involvement in your program?

STACEY: Parental involvement is an important part of the program. Parents can watch and listen to the class from an adjoining observation room and then try some new techniques at home. We talk with parents about the specific strategies that are effective with their child. Individual speech therapy is a great way to teach some skills, but I'm not really going to have much effect in thirty minutes once a week unless I'm using that time to teach the parent about things they can do the other 99% of the time. Practicing speech is not sitting down once a day for twenty minutes, not with kids this young. It's just got to be incorporated in their daily activities.

JENNIFER: One thing that I have been incredibly grateful for is the amount of help that was available and the quality of the help that was available. What would you want parents to be looking for? What would be your advice to parents?

STACEY: My advice is to listen to your gut. Listen to that vague feeling or little voice that's telling you something is not right. Even if your mother-in-law, or your pediatrician, or your sister is telling you something different, listen to your gut feeling because there is no harm in having an assessment. Get your child assessed by a specialist, an OT and/or a speech pathologist.

Your pediatrician can be a great resource, but many still have a "wait and see" philosophy when it comes to communication development. As a medical professional, a pediatrician may be more focused on general health and wellness. When you go to a specialist, that person should know an awful lot about their area of expertise. People often wonder, "How can you do a speech or language assessment on a kid who's not even talking yet?" Well, speech doesn't just happen. There are precursor skills that need to occur. Early social communication skills follow a predictable developmental pattern. And many skills need to develop before verbal communication can occur.

JENNIFER: As a speech therapist, what would be the main red flags that you would want to get assessed?

STACEY: A nine-month-old who is not babbling. A twelve-month-old who is not making speech-like sounds, playing peek-a-boo, or using a variety of gestures like pointing, giving, showing, and waving to communicate. A fifteen-month-old who does not yet say at least three words, or use a variety of speech sounds to get your attention or point to familiar objects. An eighteen-month-old who is not yet using at least fifteen words, using gestures and words together to communicate, or doing simple pretend play. A twenty-four-month-old who does not yet use at least fifty words, use two word combinations, sequence pretend play actions, or demonstrate interest in being with other children. Any of those children may be demonstrating indicators of a communication delay.

Absolute red flags are limited eye contact, limited shared enjoyment, and limited response or excessive response to sights, sounds, and other sensory information in the environment.

A great resource is a website called www.firstsigns.org. This site is concerned primarily with autism. There is a real push to try to identify autism earlier because the outcomes are dramatically improved for children when there is early intervention. But this site has loads of valuable information about communication milestones, red flags, and even resources to help you share your concerns with the pediatrician.

JENNIFER: Any last advice to parents?

STACEY: Well, there are so many things parents and professionals can do to help a child with delays or disabilities achieve their developmental goals. I think it's most important to establish a team, where a child's parents and specialists work together to form a greater understanding of a child's abilities and the techniques that can support that child's next steps. I know a lot about communication development in very young children, but I don't necessarily know as much about speech and language with older kids. And while I have a basic understanding of sensory processing and general child development, I'm not an occupational therapist or a developmental psychologist and I'm certainly not a nutritionist or a physician. I think it's important to have a team of professionals to understand how to best address your child's developmental needs. Specific areas of development don't happen in a vacuum. Who would have thought that an occupational therapist had anything to do with talking?

JENNIFER: But in our case it had everything to do with it.

STACEY: That's how you know you are getting a true picture of your child's skills and needs, with a depth of understanding about each of these areas. And part of the plan needs to be parent involvement. You can drop your kid off at therapy or at school and come pick him up, but when the parent is involved and empowered, that's when the most efficient learning is going to happen.

JENNIFER: Stacey, thank you so much. I really appreciate your time.

STACEY: Thank you. It was my pleasure.

APPENDIX C

A Conversation with Certified Early Childhood Intervention Specialist and Educator, Katie Rose, M.Ed.

JENNIFER: I'm here today talking with Katie Rose, Toby's special education teacher at our school district's preschool. Katie, thank you so much for talking with me.

KATIE: It's my pleasure.

JENNIFER: Katie, I have talked with Toby's speech therapist at Columbus Speech and Hearing Center (CSHC) about intervention before the age of three. Your school begins interventions at age three. Is there anything you would like to tell parents about later intervention?

KATIE: One thing that I would certainly say to parents is that it is never too late. You don't always see the discrepancies in development or the children may not show signs of delays until they are older. We know that with Toby that wasn't the case, but I would certainly say that it is never too late and that you can always seek out help whenever you are concerned.

JENNIFER: Yes, that's true. I think in the end it was a blessing that Toby was so severe, because we caught it so young, but I know many parents who didn't see it so early. Sometimes, the difficulty is that you live with your child every day and you are used to their behavior and often don't notice the differences.

KATIE: Right. Early intervention is key obviously and what we are doing as teachers is stressing that importance, because we know that early intervention is crucial. Researchers say that a majority of brain development occurs by age five or six. Your local, city school system is going to be your number one resource for evaluating your child and determining if there are discrepancies in his development. In addition, try considering the age that milestones were reached by other siblings or observing peers that are the same age as your child when you are at the park, local library or on play dates. You can also consult your pediatrician if you are unsure.

JENNIFER: Can you tell us a little about sensory processing issues?

KATIE: Sure. Sensory processing is the ability to process and organize information received by the senses. Children are often sensory seekers or sensory avoiders. Toby was a classic sensory avoider. He didn't want to touch or interact with textures that were messy, grainy, sticky, wet, cold, or hot. When given activities involving these sensory experiences, he would become very anxious and get upset.

JENNIFER: Yes, and he used to cry just at the sight of grass. If he went outside, even in shoes and socks and pants, just the thought that he might actually have to walk or step on grass made him cry.

KATIE: Right, and he did not want to touch sand or even step on any shifting ground, like sand, when you were on vacation. That was a significant sign and is certainly something to be aware of – how does your child respond to certain textures?

A sensory aversive child can also be a very restrictive eater. They may avoid textures that are soft, squishy, or chewy, or they may avoid the crunchy, hard types of foods like crackers. So they can be restrictive in different ways and I have seen a representation of both in my classroom.

A child who is sensory aversive may dislike a gummy bear or jello type of texture, but on the other hand, I had a student who loves those types of foods but will gag over a graham cracker.

There's a progression of support that I often use to help a child who is aversive to certain food textures or is a very restrictive eater. I first help the child to tolerate a food they dislike on his or her plate. I put it on the plate and just help the child to be able to tolerate the food being there for meal after meal. From there, the next step is to have the child smell it. For some kids, just smelling a food can be upsetting. Then from that step of just smelling the food, I encourage the child to take a lick. After the child is successful with a lick of the new food, we progress to trying a bite. I have the child try the new food several times. Children often have to taste a new food up to fifteen times before it becomes something that tastes good to them.

Toby is a child who really wants to please and he always wanted to do what we asked, even if it was sometimes pushing him outside his comfort zone. So we used a behavior modification system to get him from the point of having extreme reactions to foods to independently trying new things. We used a chart that was very motivating for him. When he tried a new food he got to mark off his "smiley face" and once he got twenty "smiley faces" we had a little party in the class.

If a parent wants to try this they could easily adapt this for the home setting. Have your child pick a motivating reinforcer as a reward for trying or tolerating a certain number of new foods.

Another concern with Toby was that his relatives found him to be very averse to touch. Children who have sensory processing disorder may be very, very aversive to people touching or hugging them. Even though they may want the affection, it is sometimes difficult for them to process that tactile input and be okay with another child or person being within their close proximity and wanting to be affectionate with them.

JENNIFER: Yes. Toby was always fine with me or Nathan, because he knew what we would do, but children especially were frightening to him. We couldn't, for example, go to a busy playground because kids are unpredictable and another child might touch him or run into him or knock him down accidentally and he found that very frightening. And so classroom situations were also hard.

KATIE: Right, and parents will sometimes say, "Well, I'm seeing my child not wanting to play with other kids," or perhaps their children get really upset when another child is in their space and they are thinking more along the lines of it being a behavior or social issue. Sometimes what you have to do is kind of peel back the layers and you might discover that it isn't a delay in social skills, but instead it is a sensory issue. It's not so much that they don't *want* to interact with others, but more that they don't want other children in their space or touching them because they cannot process that input and it is uncomfortable for them. With touch being one of the senses that is affected by sensory processing disorder (SPD), it can be very difficult and very alarming for a child to even play in close proximity with other children, let alone exchange materials or try to share.

Another sign for parents to look for is how their child responds to auditory input. A child with SPD may be extremely sensitive to loud sounds. In school, it could be the fire drill, or it could be a train going by, or an ambulance siren. On the other hand, your child may be over-tolerant and not be affected or even aware of extremely loud noises.

JENNIFER: Parades were horrifying for Toby because of the people and the loud sounds. He could cope with it if he sat on my lap, but he wouldn't enjoy it. He could do it if we sort of physically framed him in.

KATIE: Sure. I had a student who would get very upset about using a towel dispenser after washing his hands. Now the towel dispenser is not what you would anticipate as something that would set him off, because it's not extremely loud. But with children who have sensory processing disorder, and also with children who are on the autism spectrum, it's been proven that they may hear things differently. They may hear noises more loudly than what we do.

JENNIFER: When Toby was very young my main fear was that he had autism. At the time, all I knew about autism was the most extreme part of the spectrum where kids couldn't connect with people emotionally, and so I was comforted because I knew Toby loved me and I knew he would make eye contact with me as a baby. But every other symptom of autism that I was aware of, other than flapping or repetitive motion, it seemed he had – he started language but then he lost his language, he wouldn't touch things, he couldn't be comforted. I thought, "What can this be if it's not autism?" because I'd never heard of sensory processing disorder.

KATIE: Yes, and it's a hard topic because it's a more recent diagnosis and there's not a stand-alone test that gives an exact yes or no diagnosis of SPD. In addition, SPD is not a defined disorder in the DSM-IV like autism is. The DSM-IV is the psychiatric manual of criteria for mental health disorders. Autism and SPD are also related in some ways because a child who has sensory processing disorder does not necessarily have autism, but a child who has autism can also have sensory processing disorder.

Sensory processing disorder can affect so many different areas of development. It can affect your gross motor abilities because your vestibular system – the system that provides information about where your body is in space and is associated with movement – is not fully developed. For example, Toby's balance was poor, so stepping on and off uneven surfaces was difficult for him. If you are seeing your child have difficulty in this area, sensory issues can be the underlying factor.

JENNIFER: Yes, and Toby wouldn't touch anything, so, because he never used his hands, his muscles were weak. So he couldn't get dressed or put on his own coat because his muscles were too weak to pull them on and his hands couldn't grip his clothing. Those sensory issues were not isolated; sensory processing disorder doesn't just affect this one area of people's lives.

KATIE: Right. Another area of development that can be affected is visual processing. It could be difficult for a child to process a lot of motion. For some kids it's very challenging to make eye contact with other people. It is just too hard and too over-stimulating for them to be able to look you in the eye and still process what you are saying. So they may be looking in all different directions and you can't figure out why they won't look at you when you are talking to them.

JENNIFER: I want to say to parents – your child doesn't have to show all of these signs. They might show just a couple of them.

KATIE: Sure, for some kids it may just be one area that poses extreme difficulty for them. Here at school we have a profile checklist that we give to parents. We take the results in the areas of auditory, visual, tactile, vestibular, and oral sensory processing and are able to gauge if your child has a probable difference, a definite difference, or is in the typical range of development.

JENNIFER: So, can you tell us a little more about your class here?

KATIE: Sure. We can have up to eight special needs students and up to eight typical peer models in our classroom. The advantage is that our classroom environment and its experiences are similar to a kindergarten setting. So we feel that we can really prepare a child for the upcoming grades and for their future. Our ultimate goal is to help each child develop his or her skill sets and support them with those areas of need so they can go on to be successful.

JENNIFER: I was surprised at how extremely, pardon the word, normal this preschool is. I'm going to show my, I guess bias is the right word, because my friend had a son who came here before Toby did and she was telling me, "Oh, it's so great, you should send your girls as typical peers" and I remember thinking, "I don't know what they would learn in a special needs classroom." My picture of what a special needs preschool would be like was frankly wrong. I was really surprised that, one, your classroom was actually academically quite a bit better than the private preschool where my girls had gone and, two, that it was really fun just like a standard preschool. Toby came home saying things like, "I got to dress up like a fireman and we made a whole city in our class today and we got to travel around and learn about people who help." It was all the typical stuff that you do in preschool.

KATIE: Yes. Here, a typically developing preschool curriculum is implemented that incorporates the State Content Standards. Your child is being taught what they need to be prepared for and successful in kindergarten.

When we work with a child with special needs in our program, we're addressing their Individualized Education Program (IEP) goals and providing extra support as necessary. We're teaching a general education curriculum but at the same time we're also providing interventions and strategies for those students who need them to be successful.

JENNIFER: What steps would you suggest a parent take to begin the process of getting into a program such as this? How is this different than the program Toby was in through the county before coming here?

KATIE: Basically, one of the main differences between Help Me Grow and our program is age.* Help Me Grow provides intervention for children up to age three. Once your child turns three they can be enrolled in our preschool program and an IEP is written if needed. The child can have an IEP from the time they start preschool at age three through high school. If you suspect that your child may have needs or you are seeing some delays in particular areas, you'll begin by going through the referral

---

*Help Me Grow is the name of the federal program in the state of Ohio. Local names will vary.

process. I would suggest that a parent get in contact with the local head of special education in their school district.

The district will then evaluate the child in all areas of development and look at where he falls within the range of what's typical, above average, or delayed. So it's really important to use that time to be very forthcoming about what you are concerned about and what needs you think your child has.

JENNIFER: Yes, sometimes the questions don't quite match what parents are seeing or the parents may want to downplay their concerns because parents don't want their children to have issues. But it's important to be honest because, in our case, the specialists really relied a lot on what I reported from home.

KATIE: Sure. And I think that it is extremely important because, especially at such a young age, when your child may or may not be verbal, *you* are their advocate. You are the person who is providing that information. So it's better to be more open and honest than not because if you are not, what can ultimately happen is your child may not qualify for services when she may need them. If a child has a moderate delay in two areas or a severe delay in one area of development, then she would qualify for special education services in our program.

I understand that the struggle with having your child labeled is very difficult for a parent. The whole process can be very overwhelming and intimidating, but it's certainly worth it. You have to think in terms of what's best for your child. If a parent is having difficulty with coping, there are resources to help and support them. Seek out blogs or parent groups to help you understand and deal with the grieving process. But ultimately, the goal is to help your child.

JENNIFER: And by getting our son help at a young age, we actually helped him *avoid* a lot of the labels that he would have had. I realize that not every child leaves here without a label, but we were able to do that for Toby. And you know, at two years old, does a child care that he's labeled as speech delayed? No, he doesn't have any idea what that is. But by taking the help now, maybe he doesn't have to go to speech therapy in fourth grade when it might bother him.

KATIE: And that's really all it is. It's just a label that gives us as teachers, parents, or other specialists working with your child an understanding and a knowledge of what is going on. For us that only helps create a sense of compassion and understanding. If I'm not really sure what's going on then I'm playing a guessing game, but having a child formally diagnosed, whether it is sensory processing disorder or autism or ADHD, whatever it is, creates a greater understanding.

People get so concerned about the stigma that's attached to a child with an identification and they worry that the teacher is going to treat their child differently. The teachers *are* going to treat him differently in a *positive* way because having a better working knowledge of what is going on enables us to better serve and support your child in the classroom setting. In addition, this is helpful once a child transitions into kindergarten. Having a clear diagnosis helps with determining what supports and interventions may be needed in the elementary grades. I provide a report about what has been successful, different strategies we used and what challenges are still present. Sometimes the teachers even call and ask me, "Okay, we are having this difficulty, what worked for you?" It lays the foundation for both the student and teacher going forward.

JENNIFER: What a great way to put that because it is a positive.

KATIE: Sure, I want parents to know that I'm on their team. We are working together. I want them to know how I can help them.

We also offer home visits for the students on IEPs which enables us as teachers to collaborate with families as well as build rapport. Your family was so open to help, to any strategies or materials I could provide to support Toby in what was happening at home. Some parents tend to be very private and they don't want a teacher to come into their house, which is understandable. For me, I look at it as an opportunity for us to really brainstorm ideas and strategies to help the child and for me to be updated on how things are going at home. The teacher really is there to be on your side, to support your child.

JENNIFER: Those home visits were an opportunity for me to figure out what you were doing in school and what we could do at home. We're not born knowing how to deal with all these things, so the home visit was an opportunity to say, "Do you have strategies for us to use at meals? I can't get Toby to sit at the table, what should we do?" That's a real opportunity to get some practical help for your family.

KATIE: The thing I think parents need to understand is that this is a process. It's not a challenge that has one solution and will be all better in a month. In this program, we are supporting the child, but at the same time challenging her so that she continues to make progress.

Sometimes, though, a child's greatest influence is his peers. He may look around and say, "Oh, she's doing that, I wonder if I could do it?" With Toby, we realized the power of watching and then doing. Whenever we felt an activity could upset him or make him defensive, we would have him come over and sit next to a child working on that activity and Toby would watch that child first. It really relieved a lot of anxiety for him to know what was going to be expected, what it was going to look like and all that was involved with the activity. Then, after he watched, it was his turn, and he always seemed to handle it better. Sometimes children develop this anxiety of the unknown. Having that opportunity just to see and then try can help a lot.

JENNIFER: Yes, and the peer angle is very important because when Toby saw his sisters doing something, he sometimes thought, "Well, they're my big sisters, they are older than me. I can't do that, I'm too little." But when he was at school he would say, "Wow, look! That kid's finger painting and he didn't die!"

KATIE: "He made it out alive!"

JENNIFER: And also, "That kid is finger painting and he made something cool and he's having fun doing it." It wasn't just that Toby was seeing kids who were surviving; he was seeing kids who were having a good time doing something. For him that was a really powerful motivator, to be like, "Wait a minute, that kid is my age. Maybe I could do that."

KATIE: Right. And one thing we really worked on with Toby was developing coping skills to figure out what he could do in a situation where he wanted to try something, but was feeling overwhelmed.

We created a visual list of techniques to try. We can take deep breaths, we can count, we can walk away and then come back and try again. He knew when he became upset or overwhelmed that those strategies worked for him. This helped him begin to independently self-modulate his behavior. I could say to him, "Okay, what can we do? You're showing me you are upset, what can we do to calm down?" And he'd think through his options. "Okay, I'm going to take some deep breaths," or "Okay, I'm going to walk away and then I'm going to come back and try it again in a few minutes." And that's what we ultimately want the children to do, to be able to independently develop coping skills. As adults, we use some of these same strategies without even realizing it to deal with everyday life.

JENNIFER: I have a friend whose son is a sensory kid and every time he needs to calm down when he's at home, he goes outside to swing on the swing set for ten minutes. Can you tell us a little more about some of the coping strategies kids use in your classroom?

KATIE: Sure. One of the main things that we do is use a lot of visuals for the kids. We have picture representations that show the schedule so that they know what to expect for the day. So for a child who is resistant to change, or has some anxiety, the visual schedule really helps them, especially on a non-routine day. We use visuals for sequencing tasks and directives as well.

For kids who are very active and have trouble sitting during large group, we give them vestibular input by using weighted lap pads, blankets or vests. Sometimes, we may have them do "heavy work," like pushing a kid's grocery cart full of food or carrying the snack bucket to the cafeteria. Doing this gives them an opportunity to release their energy and better enables them to refocus.

JENNIFER: At CSHC they used to tell the kids, "We're all going to go push on the wall as hard as we can and see if we can move the wall" just to get some input through their muscles.

KATIE: Right. We have many sensory opportunities in the classroom for the children to use as needed. We have a rocking boat, exercise ball, sit-and-spin and a trampoline. We also often have thera-putty, playdough, shaving cream, sand and water as play choices in the room. It's important for us as teachers to recognize if a child needs a sensory break and to provide her with one that is play-based so that it is a positive experience for her. The child's challenges and behaviors will not just go away, so we need to be flexible and supportive of these interventions.

Another strategy I use is to create a reward system for the children. For example, a child with whom I may be working might be very motivated by dinosaurs. Knowing that, I might make a rewards chart that says, "I will work for…" and put up a little picture of a dinosaur. The reward of playing with his dinosaurs becomes the motivator for completing a task. If he is able to follow directions and finish the task that I have asked of him, he is positively reinforced by earning his bucket of dinosaurs to play with. The use of a visual is very powerful for young kids. In this case, it is a reminder of his goal and reward. A reward system can be used for more than one task (or responsibility at home) over a longer period of time if it is more appropriate for your child.

I also use one-minute warnings in my classroom to help kids with their anxiety about change and transition. Children often want to be mentally prepared for what is coming up next. They want to know how much time they have to, say, finish building this castle they've been working on. If I just come over and tell them it's time to go, they might respond by saying, "But wait, I wanted to finish," or they may get very upset. A simple one-minute verbal prompt can prevent a possible meltdown. This is something that I can easily do and it often makes a big difference.

JENNIFER: Katie, thank you so much for taking the time to talk with me today. Is there anything you'd like to leave parents with?

KATIE: I want parents to know that they are not alone in this process. Reach out for help and support. It will lead to positive changes! Take advantage of resources that will make you more knowledgeable about what is going on and help to connect you with others going through the same challenges. Strive to embrace the changes and know that help is available.

JENNIFER: Thanks again, Katie, and thanks for everything you did for Toby!

KATIE: You're very welcome.

A Conversation with Occupational Therapist, Karen Harpster, Ph.D., OTR/L, MOT

JENNIFER: Hi, Karen, it's great to see you again. Thanks for talking with me.

KAREN: You're welcome, it's great to see you too.

JENNIFER: I think many people are familiar with a physical therapist or a speech therapist and what they do, but perhaps they are less familiar with occupational therapy (OT). Can you explain what occupational therapy is?

KAREN: Sure. Occupational therapy basically helps people create independence in their everyday activities. For kids in school it might be poor handwriting that's inhibiting them from taking notes effectively. For a person who has just had a brain injury which affects their cognitive processing, we may work on completing their everyday tasks, such as writing a grocery list and going to the store. So we look at the person holistically and we work on whatever it is that's not functioning correctly in their everyday life experiences. It could be dressing, it could be feeding, it could be their sensory processing which, of course, is going to affect everything they do.

JENNIFER: How do most parents end up getting their children into occupational therapy?

KAREN: You're talking about diagnosis. Studies show that in the case of autism, and also often with SPD and other issues, most parents know within the first year of life that something is wrong; they don't know what's wrong but they know that *something* is, and then they bring it up with their pediatrician. Often the parents' concern is language and the pediatrician tells them to wait, because language varies in the way that it develops. Then, later, most of the parents who had noticed that something was wrong were right about it – the accuracy is very high. So the incidence of parents who notice that something is wrong but then wait for services is a problem, because the kids who do best go into early intervention.

JENNIFER: It breaks my heart because I talk to so many parents who decided to wait after seeking advice or who just couldn't find someone who would take their concerns seriously. It's why I suggest getting evaluated by an occupational therapist or a speech therapist, whichever is more appropriate, because they are going to recognize those really early signs. I didn't know of that option, and now I want to get the word out.

KAREN: Yes, I think that parents who are advocates for their child, and don't let people tell them no, are the parents who are not only going to get into services, but are also going to have the kids with the best outcomes. They are usually the parents who continue therapy practices at home, and that is so helpful.

There's not a lot of research on home programming, but we know that when parents follow through at home, we really see the changes and pretty quickly. I think parents also see sensory issues the most in their everyday routines. For example, things like bathing and dressing and eating will show more of the problems. Parents come in and tell us what's happening at home, but we don't get to see those things in therapy firsthand.

Also, I have noticed that parents don't pick up on things as quickly with their first child because they don't have a comparison. For example, in my research study there were so many kids whose parents were thinking they were typical, but they were almost two years old with just five words. And, especially with language, I think parents don't realize that's not normal. Often, if it's their first child, things might get overlooked.

JENNIFER: I can see that because, after our experience with Toby, we realized our second daughter, Rachel, probably had some mild sensory issues that we didn't recognize. Because they weren't severe, she corrected on her own, but it's interesting to look back now and notice, for example, that she really hated to have anyone brush or cut her hair and that was probably a sensory behavior.

Could you tell us a little bit about what you did with Toby?

KAREN: Sure. I started with Toby when he was about two or two and a half. Toby was the kind of kid who was really over-responsive to a lot of different senses, so he didn't like to touch messy things such as shaving cream or paint, and he didn't like when they got on his clothes. He was an extremely picky eater, and his tactile system and his oral sensory processing system were on overload a lot of the time, so he just couldn't handle things that other kids could handle. He was really sensitive with his clothing too because his tactile system was very over-responsive, so we did a lot of things to decrease his sensitivities in those areas.

A lot of times with sensitive eaters, feeding starts out being a sensory issue but can then turn into a behavior issue. So, because the children don't like certain textures or temperatures or feelings in their mouths, they avoid them. Then the avoidance becomes more of a habit and their anxiety levels increase when they have to try different things. Toby was lucky enough to get into treatment early and we could deal with that. It's easier to deal with early on, whereas when you start to see a five or six-year-old we might make great progress, but at the same time their behaviors have often overshadowed the sensory issues. It starts out as being a tactile sensitivity but then, because the sensory system is so closely related to their sympathetic system, it sometimes overpowers.

JENNIFER: So walk us through a typical hour of therapy with Toby.

KAREN: For a typical hour session with Toby we would start off by getting him ready to eat so we would do things that would get his body in a state where his anxiety level was decreased and he was calm. We would have what we call "heavy work" – proprioceptive activities like jumping or doing obstacle courses that included going through tunnels and jumping in the ball pit, climbing on walls, anything that would add some resistance or heavy work. This also helped with his gross motor and vestibular issues.

JENNIFER: Can you explain why you would do those heavy work activities, like jumping, to make him calm because my first instinct to calm a child would be to do something like play quiet music. It seems counter-intuitive that jumping would make you calmer.

KAREN: Well, the proprioceptive system is a system where your receptors are mainly within your joints and within your muscles. Someone who has a proprioceptive system that isn't functioning well doesn't really know where their body is in space. For example, when they raise their arm they're not quite sure where their arm is because their receptors aren't working; it's not registering that information. So if a person's receptors aren't telling them where their body is in space, jumping up and down gives them that heavy impact on their joints that help their receptors register the input. If they are just walking it's not going to be enough force to know where their body is.

JENNIFER: So it is almost like they need to be heavier so they can feel it?

KAREN: Exactly. That's why we use weighted vests sometimes, because it gives more weight to your body so you know where your body is in space or we use compression vests to squeeze your body so that you have extra help to know where your body is in space. It's related to the vestibular system as well. The vestibular system's receptors are in your inner ear and there is fluid in your inner ear that moves every time you move, so, for example, if you turn your head or if you jump up and down that fluid is going to move. For kids who have vestibular systems that aren't working well, that extra motion can help.

When we do linear, vestibular movement, that is calming. When we do rotary or spinning movement, that's alerting. So for a kid who needs to be calm, we want to add some kind of movement that's going to give them extra input on their joints and also move them in a line. That's why we swing a lot. And we can also use a swing that adds extra input to the joints such as a swing made from something stretchy like spandex and swing the child in a line.

Because Toby's anxiety level would get so high around eating and his sympathetic system would go into that fight-or-flight state, we would need to do some heavy work and some vestibular work to get his body back into a calm state.

With Toby we added a behavioral approach to his food therapy time so we made charts and wrote down how many new foods he had tried to give him the encouragement and the motivation to eat the foods. Once he had eaten ten foods we would have a party. Sometimes we would have a picnic on the floor. Giving Toby some control over what we were going to eat the next week also helped. We would have some foods that I knew he would eat and some that would be challenging for him so that it wasn't a completely stressful situation for him.

The other thing that we would do is play with food. For example, if we had gummy bears and yogurt we might have the gummy bear swim in the yogurt. In the beginning it was hard for Toby to touch certain types of food, so we would think of ways to make games out of it. With Toby, I could push pretty far before he would melt down, compared to some of the kids I see. You just have to get to know where each kid's thresholds are and how far you can push them.

JENNIFER: Toby had an occupational therapist at his preschool as well, but what they worked on was completely different. It was almost entirely fine motor skills, while you were able to address sensory issues and his feeding. Can you talk about why school and private therapy would look so different?

KAREN: Sure. In schools, the occupational therapy goals need to focus on school-related issues. So if a younger child doesn't know how to form his letters then they might qualify for special needs services. An older child who doesn't quite have the ability to write quickly enough to keep up with the class might get OT to work on typing. In an outpatient OT program such as private therapy, we have a lot more freedom, so we can really look at the whole picture to figure out what are the most important issues to address.

JENNIFER: What was interesting to me is that as we were able to address Toby's more "global" issues, all of the other stuff came in line. It was useful for him to have both kinds of therapy, but if I had needed to choose I would have thought that the more comprehensive, private therapy would have eventually fixed the other issues. The school therapy seemed to focus on smaller symptoms of the larger problem.

KAREN: Right. For example, motor planning is the ability to think of what you want to do, plan how you would do the activity, and then carry out that plan. In an outpatient setting I can look at how motor planning is going to affect every aspect of your life, whereas a school therapist is going to have to think about motor planning and its influence on how a child writes his letters, for example. It's just a more restrictive environment.

JENNIFER: That is one reason why we pursued private therapy in addition to the school-provided therapy. Can you give me an example of motor planning so people know what that is?

KAREN: Sure. A good example would be catching a ball and the anticipatory actions related to that. To catch a ball, you need to know where to put your body, where to put your arms, how to anticipate how far or how fast, or if the ball is going to your right and you need to move your body to the right. You can think, "Okay, the ball is going to the right, I have to move my body there, and put my hands up and then I can catch the ball." So as occupational therapists we break that down to try to figure out what part you might need help with. Is it that you don't know how to plan that action? Is it the actual performance of it, the motor actually moving your body? Is it the thought, the plan, or carrying out the action?

With sensory processing, kids improve with experience and exposure. As you are getting these experiences your body is effectively creating a map. You can really change that map. The theory behind sensory processing is that you can change the underlying neurological system and so, with repeated exposure, kids are making changes within the neurological organization in their body. We write a sensory plan so every two to three hours they are getting that input and so, with repetitive movement or action, whichever sense it is that they need, their neurological systems are changing.

We use what we call the "just-right challenge" with sensory processing. We try to plan activities that are challenging enough for the child to make that change in the neurological system. If the activities that you create are all at that child's level, if there's no challenge, there's going to be no re-mapping and that change isn't going to be made. So we plan something that is going to be a little bit of a challenge for the child but not too much. That way they can be successful and produce an adaptive response which will make the changes in their neurological system.

JENNIFER: Can you talk just a little bit about the range of what a parent might see? Toby was so completely over-responsive, but in fact that's not very common; a lot of kids have both over-responsive and under-responsive symptoms.

KAREN: Yes. It gets really complicated because you can be under-responsive in any or all of the seven systems and over-responsive in any or all of the seven systems. The seven systems are vestibular, proprioceptive, tactile, auditory, sight, smell, and taste. And the child's responses could look different in different environments. At home where the child is comfortable and relaxed, you might not see one response as much as you would in a school where things aren't as predictable.

That's why sensory processing is intriguing because it changes depending on so many different things. You really have to look at the environment and the context. Did the child sleep? Did he eat? Does he have a security blanket? Is his mom with him or is he on his own? Children might be nervous on a playground at school because other kids are running toward them and they're not quite sure how to move their bodies to avoid that situation or the noise level might be loud and that might create anxiety. There are just so many different conditions that can affect how they are going to respond to what is happening around them.

Often parents report that the kids are so good at school and then they come home and they're having tantrums and they're just "out of whack." Especially with autism that is very common, because they hold it together at school, but when they get home they are a mess; that's their safe place. So one of the recommendations that I always make for parents is that they have an hour at home after school where the child can just do whatever he wants. Have a quiet place, maybe a tent, where they can do their own thing, or a trampoline where they can jump and decompress, because they have worked so hard at keeping their sensory system together at school that they can't handle it when they go home.

JENNIFER: Can you give us some examples of symptoms that a parent might see that would be concerning, or that would be the first signs that a child might have some sensory issues?

KAREN: Sure. Some of this is geared towards early signs of autism but some of the literature on the first year of life is that kids with sensory issues don't make a lot of eye contact, they can either be over or under-responsive to sound, they might not want to cuddle with their parents so when they pick them up they might arch their back or squirm away.

JENNIFER: I have to say we didn't see any of those. Well, Toby was under-responsive to sound, but he couldn't hear.

KAREN: Well, these are definitely more early signs of autism but in a sensory processing realm. If they are picky eaters, that could be another sign.

JENNIFER: Our very first sign was that Toby would not eat solid food.

KAREN: When they get into the preschool years, two, three, four, it's a lot easier to see. If they are over-responsive you might see that certain clothes bother them, the seams in their socks might bother them, or you might notice that they are really sensitive to one temperature or another, for example at bath time. With the vestibular system, when you tilt their head back to wash their hair they might have a negative reaction, because if they are not sure where they are moving they might not be able to deal with that. Some parents report that changes of clothes from winter to summer, when they start to wear short sleeves for example, can be an issue and sometimes the light touch of the wind on their arms can be alarming. Also, they might be alarmed or startled by noises that shouldn't be startling, like the vacuum cleaner or the blender.

JENNIFER: And what would some of the symptoms of an under-responsive child be?

KAREN: They are the kids who are hard to detect. You might have to call their name several times before they respond. You might think that it's typical kid behavior, but you might have to touch them before they acknowledge that you are talking to them. Or they might just seem lazy so you will often see school-age kids that are under-responsive slumped over on their desk because they just don't have the body awareness to sit up.

Kids might stuff their mouths or be very messy when eating to try to feel the food. Also, some kids will fall a lot or run into things on purpose, or they might be under-responsive to pain. They might get a cut or a bruise and they don't react because they don't feel it like they should.

JENNIFER: What would you tell parents if they are noticing these things? How would they begin, where would they go, what would they do?

KAREN: I think to a degree it depends on where you go for services. Technically, occupational therapists don't need a referral from a doctor but some places do require referrals. So you can go to your pediatrician and ask for a referral or you can just contact a place that does occupational therapy and get an evaluation. That's really the main thing. It's not hard. The downfall is that occupational therapists don't have a lot of great sensory processing assessments. We did the Sensory Profile with Toby which is good and gives a parent a report of how the child functions within their environment and what is bothering them, but we don't have a lot of assessments for direct observation. I did the Sensory Integration and Practice Test on Toby, but Toby was a great person for that because he had a lot of verbal skills and he was cognitively aware and could do a lot of the tests. We don't have a lot of great clinical assessments yet.

JENNIFER: Please do talk about that a little bit because sensory is kind of a new thing and I know there is controversy about where it fits. Is it on the autism spectrum or is it its own thing?

KAREN: The theory has been around since the 1960's, but the problem is that we don't have a lot of good literature that supports it. So for an intervention to be highly effective you have to have randomized controlled trials that show that one group of kids got the therapy and one group didn't and then demonstrate that there are differences between the two. Well, there are a lot of reasons why we can't do that. First of all, when kids have these issues we can't withhold therapy. The other issue is that we're just not there in the research area of occupational therapy. We are starting to have some randomized control trials and we are starting to do some intervention studies, but it's not quite at the level where it needs to be to show that, "Yes, this is why this kid changed."

Some research is coming out now where we are actually doing neurological tests, so we're measuring brain waves and we're doing MRIs or fMRIs to show that there have been neurological changes *because* of what we are doing. That's really just starting now. We need to be able to show that the reason this kid can eat now is because we did this therapy.

JENNIFER: Well, it obviously worked for us with Toby. And he loved it.

KAREN: Yes, the reason I like working with kids is because it's fun. What is a kid's occupation at such a young age? It's to play. And when they can't play and explore their environment, how much is that going to affect the rest of their lives? When you have sensory processing issues and you can't crawl around on the floor to learn about how things feel or what things sound like, it really has a negative effect on the rest of your development because by *not* experiencing the environment, by *not* doing things, your brain is not developing as it should. But if we could do this intervention or teach parents how to arrange their environment so the child is getting these experiences, it can result in such a profound change.

JENNIFER: So is there anything else that you would want to share about sensory processing?

KAREN: Sensory processing really is complex and it can take a variety of forms, so, if you think that there's an issue, it's important to get your child evaluated. And when you *do* get your child therapy, you need to take advantage of learning what activities you can do throughout the week to help whatever the child's goal is. The kids who have the most success have parents who do things and set up the environment so that their children are challenged at home. With repeated exposure and knowing *why* the therapists are doing what we are doing and how the parent can do it at home, it's going to be so much more beneficial.

JENNIFER: I almost felt that therapy was more like time for you to model what Nathan and I could do at home.

KAREN: Right, but not everybody thinks that way. Actually, a lot of people don't think that way. I try to do as much as I can in that one hour a week, but really it needs to happen at home too, especially with eating and behavioral issues.

JENNIFER: With eating, oh yes. Toby would not be eating now if we hadn't done it at every meal of our lives and I don't downplay that. But to encourage parents, when you say "set up the environment to challenge them at home" I think people picture this huge production and it wasn't that at all. The only thing that we did in our house that was any different really was to put a bounce house in our basement. It was more about knowing how to handle it when our child was having a hard time. We could say, "Hey, why don't I take the cushions off the couch and make you into a sandwich and I'm going to squash you between these cushions and it's going to be funny," because he needed some physical input to his body. Or saying, "Hey, run outside and swing for a little bit," because we knew that swinging would calm him down.

KAREN: Right, it's just the little things and knowing how to respond and manage behaviors. There is almost always a reason for the behavior. It's almost always a response to something. We have to figure out why the behavior is happening and come up with a solution. Kids don't want to be bad, they don't want to have tantrums, they're acting out for a reason, and we need to figure out why.

JENNIFER: Karen, thank you so much. This was really helpful.

KAREN: You're welcome! I enjoyed it.

Suggested Online Resources for Parents

This list is meant to be a helpful starting place for parents who have concerns about their child's development. This is by no means a comprehensive list, and Jennifer has not used all of these resources, nor does she expressly endorse them. However, these have been suggested by professionals as good resources for more information on dealing with disorders such as SPD, autism, and speech delay. Websites change frequently, so please be aware that this information may become outdated.

◊ **Sensory Processing Disorder Foundation**
  - This website has an incredible amount of information including articles, classes, books, help in finding therapists, suggestions on feeding issues, and much more.
  - http://sinetwork.org or http://spdfoundation.net

◊ **National Dissemination Center for Children with Disabilities**
  - This resource covers federal laws and programs in each state, parents' rights, and has helpful information about the entire range of disabilities for all ages.
  - http://nichcy.org

◊ **Zero to Three, National Center for Infants, Toddlers, and Families**
- This group specializes in health and developmental guidelines and resources for parents, teachers, and policy makers who affect the lives of young children.
- http://zerotothree.org

◊ **The American Speech-Language-Hearing Association**
- This professional association of audiologists, speech-language pathologists, and speech, language, and hearing scientists makes information available on every aspect of communication.
- http://asha.org

◊ **First Signs**
- Covering autism and related disorders, this resource has information on early detection, screening, and referral, and even suggestions for effective ways to share concerns with your physician or another parent.
- http://firstsigns.org

◊ **Apraxia–Kids, The Childhood Apraxia of Speech Association of North America**
- This website has a wealth of information about speech delay and speech disorders.
- http://www.apraxia-kids.org

◊ **The Hanen Centre**
- The Hanen Centre specializes in speech issues with children, utilizing a family and parent-led model along with therapy to improve communication.
- http://www.hanen.org

◊ **The Columbus Speech & Hearing Center (CSHC)**

- This is the center where Toby went for toddler preschool and private OT and their website is also a wonderful resource for communication and sensory issues.
- http://www.columbusspeech.org

◊ **Help Me Grow from the Ohio Department of Health**

- Help Me Grow is the state-wide program in Ohio that helped connect Toby with CSHC. Their website has lots of information on pregnancy, early childhood development, and resources for parents and professionals.
- http://www.ohiohelpmegrow.org

◊ **Ohio Coalition for the Education of Children with Disabilities**

- A state-wide non-profit organization that helps connect parents with resources and serves children with any disability in the state of Ohio until adulthood.
- http://www.ocecd.org

J ennifer Shaw is a singer, songwriter, speaker, and worship leader whose heart belongs to the Lord. She has ministered at women's events, worship services, retreats, and concert events across the country and around the world, and she would love to be with you! For more information on Jennifer's ministry, speaking topics, and music, please find her here:

http://jennifershaw.com
http://facebook.com/jennifershawfans
http://twitter.com/shawjennifer

Thanks so much for using your gifts and talents to the glory of God - I certainly was blessed!
Joni Eareckson Tada, speaker/author/radio host

I had the privilege of ministering with Jennifer at a women's retreat and was moved by the depth and breadth of her music. Her love for and dependence on God was so evident!
Ruth Hill, Head of Women's Ministry, Evangelical Covenant Denomination

Her stunning voice, music, and personal story touched our church deeply. I recommend her heartily!
Kevin Pound, Senior Pastor, Mandarin Presbyterian Church, Jacksonville, FL

Jennifer was a true inspiration to the women who attended our event! Women were moved to a closer relationship with the Lord through her ministry.
Tina Hooper, retreat organizer, Saranac, MI

info@jennifershaw.com
Jennifer Shaw Music, P.O. Box 340773, Columbus, OH 43234